Dear Ed,
Happy 30th Birthday!
Hope this will help you
become a 2nd F. Lee Bailey!
        Love,
            mom

— Good Reading.

COURTROOM TESTIMONY

COURTROOM
TESTIMONY:★

A Policeman's Guide

by KEVIN TIERNEY, M.A., LL.M.

Funk & Wagnalls / New York

Contents

Instructions to Juries Regarding the Testimony of the
Police/ Some Indications of Jury Attitudes/ Why
Juries?/ Mistrial Where Jury Hears Inadmissible
Evidence/ Inadmissible Statements Volunteered by
Police Officers/ Waiver of Jury Trial/ Police
Officers as Jurors

8 ★ ON THE WITNESS STAND   103

Why a Witness Is Called/ The Burden of Proof/
The Right of an Accused To Remain Silent/ The
Right of an Accused To Testify/ No Inquisition in
American Law/ The Position of a Witness/ The
Sequence of Questioning/ Privilege in Court/ How
a Witness May Be Attacked/ Hostile Witnesses

9 ★ FACING OPPOSITION COUNSEL   119

Pre-Trial Aid in Preparing for Cross-Examination/
Direct Examination as a Basis of Cross-Examination/
Inconsistency/ The Source of Prior Statements/
Avoiding Inconsistency/ Use of Contemporaneous
Memoranda By Witness/ Why Lawyers Look for In-
consistency/ Sequestration/ Police Officers in the
Courtroom Who Are Not Witnesses/ Defense Tactics
in Cross-Examination/ The Power of Cross-Examina-
tion/ Games Defense Attorneys Play/ Antagonism
During Cross-Examination

10 ★ THE DEFENSE OF ENTRAPMENT   144

The Meaning of Entrapment/ *Sherman v. United*

COURTROOM
TESTIMONY

1 ★ The Police and the Courts

The police are the occupational group most frequently called upon to appear in court. Nowadays, a trial without at least one police-officer witness would be as unthinkable as a trial without a judge, and probably as ineffective. In the hundred years since the establishment of organized police forces in America, the police have come to dominate our system of criminal justice. There are other familiar participants in the courtroom scene, such as doctors, probation officers, and forensic scientists, but policemen who testify outnumber them. Furthermore, police evidence is usually more crucial than that of other occupations: in the majority of criminal trials, the public prosecutor relies on police testimony. True, the ordinary citizen who comes forward to tell his story is indispensable, and the police will never replace him, but a prosecutor depends on the police for testimony that "links" the accused to the crime.

In spite of these obvious facts, little is done to ensure that police officers will present their information competently on the witness stand. At best, they pick up some knowledge of criminal procedure from observation, but they are not exposed to any detailed explanation of strategies that are practiced daily by lawyers. This situation is indefensible. If lawyers find it worthwhile to consider their every move, police officers ought to do the same. Not only does the effective presentation of police material serve the public interest, but the legal process benefits from the good training of all its major participants.

Before the establishment of the modern police force a prosecution could be undertaken with any hope of success only if enough lay witnesses could be found. Prosecutors resorted to paying informers, and promising immunity to criminals who would incriminate their colleagues. These methods remain in use today, but have ceased to be the only method of law enforcement, because a prosecutor turns first to the police for evidence and only second appeals directly to the public. The witness stand has become the domain of the policeman.

The idea of training a witness may sound like a novel one; giving evidence in court has always been considered an amateur function, for which no special preparation was required. We might legitimately ask, however, the reason for this attitude. Is it because people believe that a witness's effectiveness cannot be improved by training, or merely because the courts must take most of their witnesses as they find them—ordinary people who have probably never stepped inside a courthouse before? Almost certainly, the latter explanation is correct. Trial lawyers find it a valuable practice to instruct witnesses for their side in advance of their cases, and expert witnesses such as doctors and forensic scientists prepare their testimony. Indeed, legal folklore advises a lawyer never to put a witness before a jury unless he himself would be convinced by his testimony.

A policeman's effectiveness as a witness can be improved by training, just as any skill can be developed. Police needs in this respect have been ignored largely because the agencies that might meet them—the prosecuting officers, the courts, the local police forces—have too many demands upon their services already. The consequence has been that police testimony has generally left much to be desired.

The difficulties of the police in the courtroom have been compounded by the peculiar development of Anglo-American law.

POLICE NEVER RECOGNIZED AS JUDICIAL ORGANIZATION

In our legal system, the police usually are not officers of the court. Only when they act in pursuance of a warrant issued for a specific purpose do they take on the status of court officials. This is an oddity, because even a bailiff— one who seizes goods in satisfaction of a civil judgment— is indeed an officer of the court and comes directly under its discipline. Many recent Supreme Court decisions that touch the day-to-day conduct of police investigation have been intended to bring the police under court control.

At one stage in history, the police were part of the judicial system; a local constable acted under the authority of local magistrates. But with the development of police departments, that connection was lost. The famous legal theorist Jeremy Bentham drew up a comprehensive plan for a judicially controlled police force and subdivided police functions into eight categories. But his plan was ignored, and the courts never took over the responsibility for enforcing their own criminal laws.

The result of American law's disassociation of the police

from the judiciary has been to create some tensions between the police and the courts. If the police were part of the court establishment, it is almost certain that the average policeman would have much more legal training than he has today. As it is, the police often feel that the courts are hindering effective law enforcement.

POLICE FORCES DID NOT EXIST
WHEN COMMON LAW DEVELOPED

The English common law from which American law is derived grew up long before the era of professional police forces. Hence, it never developed any rules dealing with the police force as an organization; common law dealt with policemen only on an individual basis, by recognizing the special status of a *constable,* who had the duty of keeping the "king's peace." A few particular rules of law grew up regarding constables, but the growth of a professional body of crime fighters was not anticipated by the common law.

In the United States today there is no coherent body of legal rules that deals with police forces. What rules there are have been produced on a case-by-case basis by the courts, and then added to by sporadic legislation. The police therefore have an ambiguous and ill-defined relationship with the criminal courts. Although most of the energies of police departments are devoted to serving the courts, they are not acknowledged as distinct legal institutions. The situation is different in many European countries, where the police have a legal status occupying a midway position between a military force and ordinary civilian organizations.

A consequence of the police developing later than the

common law has been an imbalance in the resources available to prosecution and defense. The prosecution is fed information through the police, whose investigations are financed from public funds. There is almost no limit to the amounts that may be spent in pinning down a particular crime. The F.B.I. spent well over a million dollars in apprehending the alleged murderer of Dr. Martin Luther King, Jr., and no public objection was voiced. By contrast, the defense frequently has no money to spend upon producing exculpatory evidence. A defendant may not demand that the police investigate matters upon his behalf.

Thus, although American criminal proceedings are often characterized as "adversary," it is a mistake to think that the contestants are evenly balanced. In this respect, criminal proceedings have been made more inequitable by the rise of the police force: before the police existed, both prosecution and defense operated without any substantial investigatory resources. Now, the prosecution has a formidable body of detectives to aid it.

If the public has an interest in justice, rather than wholesale conviction regardless of the guilt or innocence of particular defendants, it is not easy to justify the way in which taxpayers subsidize investigations for the prosecution, but not for the defense. The adversary system would seem to demand that the public support not only a police force, but an anti-police force; not only a prosecutor's detective squad, but a defendant's as well.

In practice, the police have always allied themselves to the prosecution and have usually been hostile, or at least indifferent, to claims made upon their time and expertise by the criminal accused. There is no necessary reason for this: it would not be incompatible with a policeman's sworn duty to uphold the law if he were to aid the defense as well as the prosecutor; the police have a duty to prevent wrongful convictions just as much as to secure rightful ones.

The historical explanation of the prosecution orientation of the police is obvious; the forces of law and order have been able to disburse tax dollars, and therefore most police forces have been beholden to their communities' governments for their very existence. This was an insignificant factor when each village and town had only one constable, but the great growth of police services and skills in the last fifty years has given a power to the prosecution that no defendant can hope to match. It may be salutary to remember what a famous defense lawyer told some Chicago prisoners during a lecture in 1902:

> If the courts were organized to promote justice the people would elect somebody to defend . . . criminals, somebody as smart as the prosecutor—and give him as many detectives and as many assistants to help, and pay as much money to defend you as to prosecute you.[1]

In other respects the prosecution may achieve an advantage over the defense purely by wielding its established power. In the well-known trial of Dr. Samuel Sheppard in 1954 for the murder of his wife, the prosecution impounded Dr. Sheppard's home from the date of his arrest until the end of his trial and refused to permit the defense to enter it. This meant that Dr. Sheppard had no means of controverting the State of Ohio's forensic assessment of the physical evidence. Almost certainly, the action of the prosecution was illegal under Ohio law. Yet the prosecution stationed a prominent police guard at the home. A writer who covered the trial commented:

Thus . . . a situation was created whereby the police were to have unlimited opportunity for leisurely examination and reexamination of the premises for evidence of Sam's guilt, while Sam's lawyers and their investigators were never, until the verdict was in, to get inside the house for even a cursory search for evidence of Sam's innocence.[2]

THE IMPORTANCE OF PUBLIC PROSECUTORS

Although law in the United States has never diverged from the common law's individualist attitude to the police, it has adopted an institution unknown in England. The common law never had a system of public prosecutors; prosecutions were started by private citizens, who swore out complaints. The only exception to this generalization was the coroner's office, which might institute a prosecution if a coroner's jury felt that the circumstances of a death justified it. In some states, the coroner continues to exercise this function and in homicide cases becomes in effect the public prosecutor.[3] A coroner is a county official who must investigate any death that takes in unusual circumstances. He has the duty to ascertain, if possible, the cause of death, and if it seems to be an "unnatural" death, resulting from criminal conduct, some jurisdictions give him the right to refer the case to a grand jury, or even to indict a suspect himself. In jurisdictions where coroners' courts still flourish, therefore, the early stages of a criminal trial may be complicated by a coroner's intervention.

However, in general in America today, prosecutions may normally be brought only through a district attorney's office. The district attorney and his assistants represent the state in all criminal matters. In some states, he is an elected official, in others he is appointed. He decides whether or not to prosecute the cases referred to his office.

Some jurisdictions do allow limited private participation in the prosecutorial process, through the institution of "special prosecutors," who are appointed in place of the public prosecutor for a particular case, and paid from private funds. This is rare today, because most members of the public have little interest in supplementing the public system at their own expense. When they have, all too often there is a personal vindictiveness involved that makes the whole practice of appointing special prosecutors objectionable anyway.[4]

Once public prosecutors were grafted onto the legal system, the position of the police with respect to legal proceedings became weaker than it had been under the common law. At common law, a policeman could institute a prosecution, not by virtue of being a constable, but because he had the same right as any citizen to do so. When public prosecutors' offices were set up, the decision to prosecute passed to the district attorney. Yet the police were not put under the control of the public prosecutor: they still remain a separate organization today, although in practice most forces cooperate closely with the local state's attorney.

This historical development removed the police further from the judicial machinery. In England, where public prosecutors have never been introduced, the discretion to prosecute remains largely in the hands of the police, and in many districts police officers actually function as attorneys: they are usually known as "prosecuting sergeants" and become highly skilled in courtroom technique. There are some courts in the United States in which policemen still fulfill the duties of a prosecutor, but they are few, and in most areas the interposition of the district attorney into the criminal process has prevented police forces from maintaining an intimate relationship with the courts.

OBSTACLES TO GROWTH OF LEGAL TRAINING

The lack of a defined relationship between police forces and the courts has discouraged the legal training of the police. There have been few attempts, until recently, to define the role of the police within the legal system. The law did not lay one down, and it was assumed to be unnecessary to provide one.

Luckily, times are changing. New courses have been developed across the country that cater specifically to the needs of an educated police establishment. Nevertheless, law enforcement syllabi have reflected an uneasy compromise among the liberal arts, law, and forensic science.[5] All these components are valuable, but they are not enough. Policemen have need of training and texts designed particularly for them, besides courses borrowed from other faculties. In particular, police officers need materials dealing with the legal process. A policeman's relationship to the courts is inevitably different from that of a lawyer or litigant. As a recent writer has said, "proper police training should . . . devote appropriate emphasis to the subject of making the policeman a good witness." [6]

There have, of course, been other obstacles to legal training. The police have, for example, been hampered by the localism that pervades police services in the United States. The federal system produces wide variations between the states, and in turn the states do not have unified police forces. On the contrary, variations within the states are often as great as those among them. As the President's Commission on Law Enforcement remarked: "Every village, town, county, city and State has its own criminal justice system, and there is a Federal one as well. All of them operate somewhat alike. No two of them operate precisely alike." [7]

The result has been gross inefficiency. Police records have not been shared; adjoining communities have widely varying standards of police protection. Insofar as the battle against crime is being lost, a major cause has been a lack of coordination between police forces on an inter- and intrastate basis. In 1963, when the "Boston Strangler" investigations were underway, a girl was found dead in Cambridge, just across the Charles River from Boston. Many features of her death were similar to those of the Boston victims. Yet the Cambridge murder was investigated by the Cambridge police, who are entirely separate from Boston. By the time there were eleven similar stranglings in the Boston area, six distinct police departments were involved, none of which was pooling information with the others. [8]

The segmentation of police endeavor in America has made it almost impossible to foster a consensus about the legitimate courtroom functions of the police.

THE LEGAL FRAMEWORK

As we know, a policeman is essentially just like any citizen in the eyes of the law; some statutes have given policemen certain powers beyond those of a private individual, but these rules are exceptional. Generally, a police officer cannot be said to have a special status before the law, such as that which diplomats from foreign countries are accorded. Thus, many of a policeman's official actions are judged by the standards that govern an ordinary citizen.

In most cases, the standard which the courts apply is *reasonableness*. This standard is at best a difficult one to define, for a policeman often finds himself in unusual situations in which no one knows what is reasonable. What should he do when threatened by a dangerous criminal? For most people, the question never presents itself in practical terms; for a policeman, it is likely he will have to answer the question more than once and frequently have to act in a split second. The courts, considering events in a calmer light, cannot put themselves into a policeman's place in the face of danger. Hence, reasonableness is a very rough-and-ready test. In a sense, the police are more important interpreters of the criminal law than the courts, because it is the police who have to decide what generalized legal rules permit in real life.

But however inadequate this legal test may be, it is better that *some* standards should apply than that control should be given up entirely. No police system can be given complete freedom of action. If everyone were locked up, it is possible that crime could be eliminated entirely; yet no reasonable person would permit the government to put such a plan into action.

It has always been difficult to know how to police the police. The law and its administration are designed to define in practical terms instances in which the end of law enforcement cannot be said to justify the means. Where that line is drawn depends on many factors, one being the mood of the community. It is generally agreed that the sixties in America were a period of deep suspicion of the police, and the result was curtailment of police activity to a considerable extent.

There is probably no perfect compromise between the demand for law and order and the demand for liberty. There will always be room for disagreement about the legal standards expected from the police. But it is clearly the duty of a professional policeman to work as effectively as he can within the legal system as he finds it. He may hold strong views about the necessity for reform, but like all professional people he is bound to acknowledge that the community's rules are more important than his personal opinions.

THE IMPORTANCE OF POLICE TESTIMONY

This book is concerned with testimony in criminal trials. Courtroom testimony is an important kind of *proof* (anything that the courts will hear that induces belief), since a prosecution is pointless unless there is a reasonable chance of obtaining a conviction. "The policeman must constantly remind himself that convictions can only be based on evidence and that it is his job to collect that evidence in a form that will support a conviction." [9]

Today, for all the scientific advances made in forensic investigation, the impressions of human beings remain the single most important type of proof that may be offered. Of course, testimony is not the only kind of evidence that a court may accept. It may view *real evidence,* which includes any physical object that is relevant to the issue before the court. It may see *documentary evidence* if that is relevant. But even these types of evidence can rarely aid the court unless they are explained by testimony, and it is therefore true to say that testimony is the most important form of proof that comes before our courts. Thus, the study of effective courtroom testimony becomes a study of effective prosecution. Since police officers are frequently required to be witnesses, they should be professionally trained for this duty.

THE PURPOSE AND SCOPE OF THIS BOOK

The purpose of this book is to improve the professional competence of police officers within the framework of the law as it stands. It deals with the special problems that arise when a police officer must himself give evidence and also covers the general subject of courtroom testimony; a witness who understands the total courtroom context can make sure his testimony has maximum impact.

A distinguishing feature of all professions is an emphasis upon technique. The fact that the legal system under which the police work may not suit them should not deter their best efforts to succeed within the system. If a police officer is occasionally frustrated in his job, he shares that fate with many people in responsible positions. If he has ideas for improvement, he is in an influential position to lobby for them. A modern officer at least cannot complain that the public does not care about his work; on the contrary, there can have been no time in the past when the role of the police has been more vigorously debated. More money is being invested in police functions than ever before, and the standing of the police profession will rise as training improves.

A notable development of the last few years is the emergence of the police as a body of trained experts. An officer with a diploma or degree qualifications in police science is now in demand from employers across the land. The President's Commission on Law Enforcement has recommended that "the ultimate aim of all police departments should be that all personnel with general enforcement powers have baccalaureate degrees." [10] No longer is it assumed that a policeman must be a local boy; he can train for his police job in California and get a job in Illinois. If there were not a growing realization that a policeman is a professional, such nationwide employment opportunities would not exist. Police education is beginning to break down the localism that has plagued police services throughout the United States.

Nevertheless, it is clear that local differences do exist and that the independent legal systems of the states will survive. This book recognizes the inevitable existence of regional variation, while attempting to surmount it for teaching purposes. It is obviously impossible to deal with the legal rules of each state individually. Thus, these pages describe legal practices in general terms; a state police officer should turn to the penal code of his own state after reading this book.

Today is not an easy time to be a policeman. In many forces, pay, administration, and training are bad, while the demand for protection in the community grows larger. At the same time, the professional advice available to those accused of crime is increasing in quantity and quality. In such conditions, it is right that books should be written about the legal process from a point of view sympathetic to the growth of police professionalism.

THE FREQUENCY OF POLICE TESTIMONY

Without police testimony, the American legal system could not function. The need for it is illustrated by recent figures. Of 1,191 criminal cases studied, the police provided testimony in 78 percent. In 98 percent of drunken-driving prosecutions, the police gave evidence. They also gave evidence in 91 percent of burglary prosecutions, 90 percent of homicide trials, 86 percent of narcotics cases, 72 percent of assaults and 60 percent of rapes prosecuted. In addition, the police, or police agencies, provided 6 percent of expert witnesses for the prosecution.[11]

Even these staggeringly high figures do not measure the full importance of police testimony. The figures relate only to the number and percentage of police witnesses; they do not measure the relative importance of what the police say. In practice, police testimony is frequently the decisive evidence, without which a prosecution could not succeed. Of special significance here is the testimony provided by the police in murder trials. Murder victims cannot speak for themselves, whereas in prosecutions of assaults that have stopped short of homicide 94 percent of complainants testify for the prosecution. It is probably a fair assumption that in modern conditions no homicide prosecution could succeed without police testimony. In this, the most disquieting of all crimes, the public is almost wholly dependent on police testimony.

In the face of these statistics, the training of police personnel for court appearance must be of the highest priority. Police testimony does not merely affect individual cases; it is the lifeblood of the whole criminal justice system.

NOTES

[1] Clarence Darrow, *Attorney for the Damned* (New York: Simon & Schuster, 1957), p. 12.

[2] Paul Holmes, *The Sheppard Murder Case* (New York: Bantam Books, 1962), pp. 37–38, 181–183.

[3] As in the Sheppard murder trial; see Paul Holmes, *op. cit.*, pp. 29, ff.

[4] See Adela Rogers St. Johns, *Final Verdict* (New York: Bantam Books, 1964), p. 357, for a case in which a private citizen paid more than $200,000 for the expenses of a special prosecutor at the turn of the century.

[5] Some "training programs" were quite absurd. In the District of Columbia, a trainee was credited with a four-hour course during which "class members donate blood on a voluntary basis." See the *President's Commission on Crime in the District of Columbia, Report on the Metropolitan Police Department* (Washington, D.C.: Government Printing Office, 1966), p. 35.

[6] H. D. Wendorf, "Police Education and the Law of Evidence" 17 *Baylor Law Review* 245 (1965), at 265.

[7] *The Challenge of Crime in a Free Society* (New York: Avon Books, 1968), p. 70.

[8] Gerold Frank, *The Boston Strangler* (New York: Signet Books, 1967), pp. 66, 92–93.

[9] H. D. Wendorf, *op. cit.*, p. 247.

[10] *The Challenge of Crime in a Free Society, op. cit.*, p. 279.

[11] Harry Kalven, Jr., and Hans Zeisel, *The American Jury* (Boston: Little, Brown, 1966), pp. 137, 140, 142.

2 ★ The Courts

A criminal trial may be *summary* or *upon indictment*. A summary trial is one before a magistrate, or other junior judge, without a jury. The courts in which such cases are heard are often referred to as "police courts," but this name is misleading, for it implies that the police control the courts, which they do not. The offenses that may be tried summarily tend to be the less serious ones.

A trial upon indictment must be before a judge and jury; the more serious crimes are tried with a jury.

In legal theory, summary trial and trial upon indictment are governed by the same rules of procedure and evidence. In practice, however, some magistrates' courts display a laxity that is a disgrace to justice.

THE LOWER COURTS

Little will be said in this book about the lower courts, which administer summary trials. Although they are more numerous than other courts and deal with a greater volume of cases, few of them ever hear a case in any detail; they dispense, as the President's Commission on Law Enforcement put it, "assembly-line justice." [1]

CRIMINAL JURISDICTION

There is a distinction to be made between federal and state crimes. Broadly, the criminal law is administered by the states. Each state of the Union has its own criminal enactments. Over acts that occur within its territory, a state has "jurisdiction"—i.e., its courts may try any criminal proceedings arising out of the acts. No other state may. Thus, if a murder is committed in Connecticut, New York State courts may not try the case; they have no jurisdiction.

Special problems arise when the elements of a crime are committed in more than one state. For example, suppose a man standing on the border of North Carolina shoots and kills a man on the other side, in Tennessee. Which state may try the man? It was held in a case where this happened that only the victim's state—Tennessee—had jurisdiction.[2] In general, such problems are rare and can be ignored in the day-to-day life of a policeman.

Apart from state criminal laws, there are federal crimes. Congress may create an offense so long as it has some relation to the execution of a power of Congress as set forth in the Constitution. Such crimes are only triable in federal courts, unless the act by which the crime was created makes some other provision.

court decides if the accused is guilty or not guilty.
chosen from the jury panel through the process of
discussed in Chapter 7, pages 82–86), comes to its
after hearing evidence, the arguments of prose-
defending lawyers, and the instructions of the

ial court acquits the defendant, the process is at an
ere is a conviction, there are at least two further
sible.

G

ty is nowadays normally determined by the judge.
there are states in which, for some or all offenses,
xes sentence. In Illinois, for example, the jury in a
se decides whether the death penalty will be im-
en where this rule prevails, however, the judge
ally sentence the prisoner after the jury's verdict.[4]

viction, a defendant may appeal. His appeal will
the state appellate court, and if it is rejected there,
ply to the Supreme Court of the United States if
itutional issue is involved. The Supreme Court has
on whether to permit an appeal or not. If it re-
conviction and sentence affirmed by the state ap-
rt stand.

ppeal court (state or federal) finds in favor of the
there are two possible consequences: either the

THE PROGRESS OF A CASE
THROUGH THE COURTS

The hierarchy of criminal courts varies from state to state,
but the broad pattern is similar throughout. A police officer
should know the channels through which a felony case must
travel. This outline traces the steps in the criminal process
through which a case must go from arrest onward:

APPEARANCE BEFORE A MAGISTRATE

A person who has been arrested must be brought before a
judicial officer (usually called a magistrate) as soon as practicable. The purpose of this rule is to prevent "police detention"; there is a fear that unless a prisoner is produced before a court quickly, he may suffer mistreatment in the
hands of the police.

At this hearing, the arresting officer will normally be
called upon to explain his reasons for arresting the prisoner.
These he should give in a normal conversational manner,
without embellishment. The standard of "probable cause"
will usually apply. However, at this stage it is unlikely that
the magistrate will inquire into the sufficiency of the policeman's reasons. His major concern will be to set bail. In most
states, bail is at the discretion of the magistrate, and the
modern trend is to grant it in all cases where there is no
overwhelming reason not to. Often, it is nowadays granted
without surety. The only cases in which it is not granted are
capital ones.

The appearance before a magistrate after arrest is common to all American jurisdictions, but from that point on,

there are varying practices. In some states, there is a preliminary hearing before a magistrate, whereas in others there is a grand jury hearing. Both are designed to produce a formal indictment.

GRAND JURY OR PRELIMINARY HEARING

In most Eastern states, the suspect must be subsequently indicted (i.e., formal charges must be made against him) by a grand jury. This comprises a number of citizens who are drawn together to decide whether the evidence in possession of the public prosecutor justifies going to trial. Although the public prosecutor has considerable influence over his grand juries, he cannot force them to return an indictment; the decision finally lies with the grand jury. In most Western states, the grand jury does not exist. In its place is a preliminary hearing before a magistrate, who listens to the prosecution evidence and who decides whether the evidence justifies further prosecution. However, in many states a defendant may "waive" a preliminary hearing, in which case the public prosecutor simply "lays an information." Upon that information, the magistrate issues an indictment.

It is doubtful whether grand juries are necessary or desirable today. They were inherited from the English legal system, from which nearly all American criminal law derives. However, grand juries were abolished in England in 1933 with no ill effects, and it is questionable whether they have not outlived their usefulness; those states that do not have the institution seem to manage well enough.

From the point of view of a police witness, there is a crucial difference between proceedings that start before a grand jury and those that start with a preliminary hearing. A grand

jury proceeding is secre
cluded and the accused
present. By contrast, a p
in open court and the ac
cross-examine the prosec
where grand jury indict
nesses are not subject to
there has been a prelimi
fronted the defense once

This has advantages
prosecutor knows in adv
under pressure on the st
must face.

ARRAIGNMENT

Once an indictment has
accused in open court.
ment, and is the beginn
accused's guilt. In some
arraignment; in others,
motions. These motions
defendant's counsel, obj
tion has indicated its int
with before trial in an
begins, it is not interrup
practice, however, even
permitted, trials rarely p
out some defense motior
fense counsel cannot po:
may object to in the pros

TRIAL

The trial
The jury,
voir dire
conclusio
cuting an
judge.

If the t
end. If th
stages po:

SENTENCI

The pena
However,
the jury f
murder c
posed. E
must forn

APPEAL

After con
first be to
he may a
any Cons
discretio
fuses, the
pellate co

If any :
defendan

defendant will go free—his conviction has been converted by the appeal into an acquittal—or there will be a retrial. When the appellate court orders a retrial, it is still possible that at the defendant's second trial he will be convicted.

The law upon retrying a defendant who has successfully appealed from conviction is somewhat confused. At common law, there could be no retrial, because there was no appeal whatever from a conviction; it was final. There has always been a principle by which a defendant is not to be put "twice in jeopardy" for the same offense.[5] However, the United States courts have adopted some form of appeal in all jurisdictions. Where a convict appeals, it is assumed that he has waived his protection against retrial,[6] but this is a dubious assumption. If a convict has his conviction quashed on appeal, it is because the appellate court finds something wrong with the trial proceedings. If there was something wrong, it will not be the defendant's fault. Why should he be re-tried because the trial court has made a mistake? Where a plea of entrapment (see Chapter 10) is entered, on the ground that police conduct has been wrong, no retrial is permitted.

TESTIMONY BEFORE THE GRAND JURY

In states in which grand juries exist, the prosecutor attempts to make out his case sufficiently strongly for the jury to indict. In practice, this is not difficult for him to do; grand juries are notoriously pliable in prosecutors' hands.

In order to convince the jury to indict, a prosecutor will normally produce some of his star witnesses, and therefore a police officer may find himself testifying before it. The prosecutor will run through the questions that he thinks will elicit facts regarding the suspect's guilt. However, he will be much less constrained before the grand jury than he will be at trial, because the rules of evidence (see Chapter 3) do not apply in grand jury proceedings; the Supreme Court has held, in *United States v. Costello*, 350 U.S. 359 (1956),[7] that an indictment based entirely upon hearsay evidence is valid. Thus, a prosecutor can throw caution to the wind.

A police officer will therefore be free to indicate to the jurors a great variety of matters that he will not be able to retell at trial. He should press this advantage in order to ensure indictment of the suspect. However, he should not assume that because the grand jury was convinced to issue an indictment the trial jury will be so easily persuaded. Not only will the rules of evidence exclude some of the materials given to the grand jury, but the standards of proof required by the grand jury and the trial jury are different. The grand jury needs only to be convinced that there is enough reason for suspicion to justify a full trial. The trial jury, of course, must be convinced of the defendant's guilt "beyond reasonable doubt."

ADMINISTRATIVE TRIBUNALS

Occasionally, a police officer will be called to give testimony outside a courtroom. A variety of administrative tribunals have powers to compel the attendance of witnesses. Administrative tribunals are set up by statute to deal with various subjects in which the government must exercise its discretion. Administrative tribunals may grant hearings relating to the grant or revocation of a license, the deportation of an alien, or any number of other problems that have been entrusted to subordinate government agencies.

Like grand juries, administrative tribunals are not bound by the rules of evidence. They may, and often do, ask for opinions from witnesses who appear before them. The whole atmosphere of administrative proceedings is less formal than that of a criminal court.

A police officer will rarely be called upon to give evidence before such tribunals. In the event that he does, he will have no difficulty if he gives his evidence as if appearing in court; if the tribunal requires further elaboration that might be inadmissible in court, it will be elicited by questions that will indicate when it needs a fuller answer than an officer has given.

NOTES

[1] *The Challenge of Crime in a Free Society* (New York: Avon Books, 1968), p. 318.

[2] See *State v. Hall,* 19 S.E. 602 (1894).

[3] See Jerry Giesler, *Hollywood Lawyer* (New York: Pocket Books, 1962), p. 249.

[4] As in the Speck trial; see Jack Altman and Marvin Ziporyn, *Born to Raise Hell* (New York: Grove Press, 1968), p. 242.

[5] See "Twice in Jeopardy" 75 *Yale Law Journal* 262 (1962).

[6] *Bryan v. United States,* 338 U.S. 552 (1950).

[7] See also Abraham Goldstein, "The State and the Accused" 69 *Yale Law Journal* 1149 (1960), at 1171.

3 ★ The Nature of the Rules of Evidence

In many countries professional judges decide matters of fact as well as law, but here nearly all serious crimes are tried by jury, and the determination of fact is the jury's exclusive province.

The use of juries is a remarkable act of faith on the part of the legal system. Jurors are expected to follow the often complex court proceedings even though they have no training whatever. In all states juries decide the question of guilt or innocence; in some, they also decide the penalty. (The President's Commission on Law Enforcement has recommended the abolition of the jury's right to decide penalties.)

The American system therefore places great trust in juries. Yet although we trust them, we do not trust them completely. The rules of evidence are a measure of our reservations about juries; if we had absolute confidence in juries, there would be no need for rules of evidence, except perhaps those that forbade a defendant from deliberately wasting the court's time. Most evidentiary rules are designed to *prevent* juries from hearing the whole truth, for fear that they would place undue reliance upon certain kinds of information. The most notorious example of such a rule is the one that prevents a jury from hearing about an accused's previous convictions. The reason for this rule is our fear that jurors will too readily convict a man if they know he has been convicted previously. That may be so; but if we had complete faith in a jury's judgment, we would allow it to have all relevant facts at its disposal.

The importance of understanding the duality of our attitude toward jurors is immense. A police officer who is to give testimony must realize that he probably knows more about the accused than the jury does. He will have a knowledge of the accused's reputation, character, past conduct, and even past admissions of crime which is denied to the jury. Consequently, he must also be acquainted with the nature of evidentiary rules.

If sometimes jurors seem to give unwise acquittals, they may do so because the court has, in accord with rules of evidence, kept them ignorant of facts well known to the police.

THE EFFECT OF RULES OF
EVIDENCE UPON TRIAL STRATEGY

If there were no rules of evidence, many more convictions would be registered than are at present. The present jury acquittal rate is about 30 percent in serious crimes.[1] If juries knew the character of some accused persons, they would almost certainly have less inhibition about convicting. Thus, most rules of evidence benefit the defense, rather than the prosecution. This, of course, is as it should be, because a defendant ought to be entitled to "the benefit of the doubt."

Strategically, a defense lawyer has, therefore, an interest in pleading that rules of evidence forbid the admission of as much of the information in the hands of the prosecutor as possible; the less the jury really knows about an accused the better, from his point of view. The reason for this is simply that most accused persons taken to court are guilty.

WHAT A DEFENSE ATTORNEY CAN HOPE FOR

The possibilities open to defense counsel are limited because the overwhelming majority of his clients are guilty; that is why he frequently resorts to "plea-bargaining." If a case is going to trial, he can hope for one or more of the following things:

That the prosecution fails to convince the jury "beyond reasonable doubt";

That he succeeds in getting some of the prosecution's proffered evidence ruled inadmissible, so that the prosecution cannot tell its whole story, and the jury acquits;

That although the trial judge admits prosecution evidence that the defense wishes to have excluded, and therefore the jury convicts, an appeal court will rule the trial judge wrong and reverse the conviction.

With these possibilities in mind, defense counsel will naturally devote a great deal of his effort to objecting to offers of evidence from the prosecution. When questions relating to the admissibility of evidence are argued, the jury is sent outside the courtroom, so that it will not know what legal arguments are submitted. This is one of the reasons that trials are unpredictable in length; until a point arises no one knows that defense counsel intends to argue it.

THE "SEARCH FOR TRUTH"

An American trial is often described as "a search for truth." It is nothing of the kind. The court hears only what it is allowed to hear, which excludes a great deal of relevant evidence. Either prosecution or defense may choose, without reference to the court, to conceal material facts in its possession. The defense of insanity is an example of this. It is entirely up to the defense whether to raise the issue of the accused's sanity; often, since most serious crimes are committed by persons who are psychologically abnormal, the decision is a close one. Yet if the defense chooses not to plead insanity, there will normally be no evidence relating to the accused's mental state. The defense is fully entitled to make its choice to keep the evidence of mental abnormality away from the court. Such a choice was made by defense counsel for Richard Speck.[2] Yet if the courts were interested in "truth" in any absolute sense, they would hear about the accused's mental state whether the parties pleaded it or not.

In this respect, Russian criminal procedure makes more provision for getting at the "truth" in the ultimate sense than does American law:

Upon indictment, the [Russian] trial commences with the court's interrogation of the accused directed . . . to his entire biography. Whether or not he is a Party member, whether or not he has been in trouble before, whether or not he has earned rewards for outstanding achievement of any kind, whether or not he took an honorable part in the Great Fatherland War—these and similar questions make it clear that it is not simply the offensive act that is to be punished or exonerated, but the man himself.[3]

No such inquiry may be instituted by a court in this country. Most of the matters that are listed above as being considered by the Soviet courts would be known as "character" evidence in the United States. Unless an accused chooses "to put his character in issue"—i.e., expressly or by implication to claim during the trial to be of good character—the court will never hear about "the man himself," but will merely deal in narrow terms with the particular crime alleged against him.

This is how a distinguished non-lawyer described the effect of American criminal procedure, and the exclusionary rules of evidence:

> Today the prime qualification for service on a jury is complete ignorance of the circumstances of the crime and of the persons involved in it. Jury trial has become a carefully staged combat between two sets of skilled attorneys, each set primarily concerned, not with establishing the truth about the crime, but with limiting and distorting the evidence in the way best calculated on the one side to convince the jury that the defendant is guilty, on the other to convince the jury that he is innocent . . . it is scarcely too much to say that the real task of the jury is to guess . . . which set of attorneys has been the most adroit in confusing the witnesses and clouding the issue.[4]

This entertaining and forthright commentary is perhaps overdrawn. In particular, it is not true on the whole that both sides wish to confuse witnesses and cloud the issue. That is the interest of the defense; since prosecutors usually have a strong case, they can rest content with presenting their evidence quite clearly.

CONTRADICTIONS IN THE LAW OF EVIDENCE

It is well known that evidence of previous convictions is usually excluded from criminal trials. It is not so well known that there are exceptions to that rule. For example, previous offenses may be proved (whether they have resulted in conviction or not) if they are similar to the one at present charged and therefore show a consistent course of criminal conduct. This is known as "similar fact" evidence. Thus, if X is charged with murdering his third wife by poison, it is permissible to show that he poisoned his first two wives.

Such evidence must be at least as prejudicial as proof of any other conviction, yet the law admits it. The jury is most likely to convict in such a case because of the disclosure of previous character. The legal justification for this exception to the rule excluding previous convictions from evidence is that proof of similar facts proves motive and intent and therefore is not introduced merely to prejudice the defendant. This is not much protection to the accused, however, for regardless of the *reason* for introducing the evidence of similar facts, the *effect* upon a jury is going to be prejudicial.

Some legal commentators have expanded the exceptions to formulate another general rule. They say that although previous convictions cannot normally be introduced into evidence, they may be if the purpose of doing so is something other than showing that the defendant has a criminal streak in him. The philosophy of the courts which accept this view is that they will permit such prejudicial matter to get before a jury, providing some appropriate legal excuse can be given for it.

There is therefore a contradiction in this rule of evidence, as in many of them. A good prosecutor will obviously manipulate the rules of evidence as far as possible in order to get in such prejudicial evidence, and, naturally, defense attorneys will object. But a police officer should note that in spite of all the concern with prejudice that the courts show, they will shrug off their scruples if given a sufficient reason to do so.

NOTES

[1] Harry Kalven, Jr., and Hans Zeisel, *The American Jury* (Boston: Little, Brown, 1966), p. 56.

[2] Jack Altman and Marvin Ziporyn, *Born to Raise Hell* (New York: Grove Press, 1968), p. 227.

[3] Harold J. Berman, *Justice in the U.S.S.R.* (New York: Vintage Books, 1963), p. 306.

[4] Carl L. Becker, *Freedom and Responsibility in the American Way of Life* (New York: Vintage Books, 1960), pp. 90–91.

4 ★ Getting to Trial

The most striking fact about criminal justice in America is that the courts play only a "window-dressing" role. Although they are the visible parts of the system, they are no longer its most influential parts. Behind the scenes, in entirely unofficial ways, the majority of cases are deflected from courtroom trial. A measure of the disassociation between courts and the general process may be gathered from the phenomenon of "plea-bargaining." This procedure, by which a public prosecutor makes a deal with a defense attorney, is wholly illegal. If the accused pleads guilty to a lesser charge that he might be tried for, the prosecutor agrees to "fix" the sentence with the judge. Not only is this highly improper, but the result is deliberate dishonesty on the part of the prosecutor and judge; when the accused pleads guilty (thereby honoring his side of the illegal bargain), the court is told that no negotiations have taken place.[1]

There are other discrepancies between theory and practice in our criminal justice system.

THE RARITY OF FULL TRIAL

It is exceptional for a case to come to trial. Much effort is directed toward case disposal without resort to the judicial process. The police frequently prefer to deal with cases by informal warning, or by obtaining a compromise plea of guilty. There has been much academic criticism of this phenomenon recently, yet there seems no alternative as long as crime rates remain high and the courts remain overcrowded. The police, in developing means of avoiding the courts, have responded naturally to their ever increasing work load; in this, they suffer from the same pressures as many district attorneys' offices.

A full trial is a cumbersome proceeding, in which many police hours must be invested. It involves extensive searches for judicially acceptable evidence, and witnesses spend long hours waiting to be summoned to testify. Since the police provide much courtroom testimony, they are particularly susceptible to inconvenience from full trials. As the Law Enforcement Commission noted, policemen must often "appear on their own time, and in their case delay has a direct effect upon law enforcement in the field." [2]

Yet apart from the practical impetus to extrajudicial means of case settlement, many police departments seek to avoid courtroom appearance because of reservations they have about the way many trials are conducted. The police know that in some state courts the judges are, or can be, bought. They know that the lawyers involved in criminal trials are often not of the highest integrity. Above all, they know that the trial process allows some suspects to be wrongly acquitted.

If a case reaches trial, the police have a vested interest in conviction; the time spent in obtaining evidence against an accused is much greater than that required for less formal case disposal, such as police warning. In many cases, the time lost because the judicial process ties up officers who must be ready to testify in court is even greater. From the police point of view, a prosecution can be justified only by conviction; otherwise, the police have wasted their time in entering the judicial arena. A criminal trial is as much a trial of the police department's reputation as it is of the defendant's guilt.

Although the police have a vested interest in the conviction of those who are brought to trial, their interest has limitations. The police should not desire conviction at any price, for no one has an interest in convicting the innocent. Rather, they have an interest, once the decision to prosecute has been taken, in *efficient* prosecution. If, in spite of the best efforts of police and prosecutor, the accused is acquitted, no harm is done. No formula has been invented that will guarantee the success of a prosecution; if it had been, the courts would merely act as rubber stamp to the prosecutor's decision to proceed against an accused. In the absence of a guarantee that prosecution will be successful, marginal cases frequently never get to court.

Faced with these realities, many police forces welcome the chance to deal with cases before they reach trial. They believe that by making a deal with the underworld, they may serve the public interest better than by going to law.

Many people have regretted that the police feel this way. But it is a natural consequence of their belief that the people they prosecute are guilty. True, they believe it on evidence that may be weaker than that required by a court, but then not many popular opinions could be proved beyond reasonable doubt; insofar as policemen have a lower practical standard of proof, they share a universal human failing. It is a principle of justice that any doubt that appears at trial should be resolved in favor of the accused. But the police know that whether or not a doubt appears often has little to do with the merits of a case; it is fortuitous if in any particular instance the police can amass absolutely watertight evidence. Indeed, the more professional a criminal is, the less likely it becomes that he will leave proof. For this reason, big-time criminals tend to have a practical immunity from the law.

Although the police understandably wish to see those whom they believe to be guilty convicted, they should remember that their judgment is not infallible. In the famous and disturbing study *Convicting the Innocent,* which was published in 1932, twenty-one out of sixty-five miscarriages of justice were attributed by Professor Borchard to the overzealousness of the police.[3] Admittedly, in nearly all of those cases, the police were acting in good faith, but it must give any thoughtful policeman pause to consider that now, nearly forty years later, conditions that permit innocent men to be convicted still exist.

Criticism of case disposal outside the courtroom is of a somewhat schizophrenic variety. The substantive law of nearly all American states permits compromise with criminals. If a self-confessed criminal will agree to testify on the government's behalf, he may be given immunity from prosecution for his own crimes. This practice is known as "turning state's evidence." Such bargains have the approval of the law, and this practice rarely receives the critical attention that unofficial police compromises have had in recent years.

Much of this critical attention comes from lawyers who rarely come into contact with the total problem of crime containment; their knowledge of criminals is confined to those who are unlucky enough to have reached the stage at which they will be tried.

Whatever moral objections may ultimately be made to court avoidance, it represents a major part of police and prosecution effort. In statistical terms, the courts are the final destination of only a small number of the cases that the police handle. The practice does raise important questions: If compromise is to be tolerated, are the police qualified to achieve it? Or the district attorneys? Or the courts? There is no doubt that the police see more of the underworld than do either the prosecutors or the courts; the criminal community and the police live in much the same world. They are engaged in perpetual symbiosis, and therefore the police have a strong claim to be the best qualified agency of compromise.

GUILTY PLEAS

The few cases that reach the courts represent only the tip of the criminal iceberg. But the majority of cases dealt with in the court do not receive full trials; they are disposed of by pleas of guilty. If the defendant pleads guilty, the standards of proof required by the courts are reduced greatly; his admission of guilt is treated as virtually conclusive. It is normal for the prosecution to make a short statement of the facts leading to the defendant's apprehension, but no witnesses are called. Some jurisdictions do not accept guilty pleas without asking questions designed to elicit whether the plea is voluntary and the defendant understands the nature of the charge.[4] However, by the time a defendant has gone so far into the process as to be interrogated by the court, it is unlikely that anything he says will reveal a defect in the plea.

This is particularly true where the defendant has a lawyer, because he will have been prepared in advance for the court's inquiry. One text for defense attorneys advises: "Of course, while the defendant must be advised of the questions and the answers expected, those answers must be truthful and not made simply to persuade the court to accept the plea."[5] In reality, it is almost inevitable that the answers will be made simply to persuade the court to accept it; the accused is probably pleading guilty because his attorney has advised him to.

It is known that mentally disturbed people sometimes confess to crimes that they did not commit. It may therefore seem strange that the courts are satisfied to take the accused's word for his guilt, but that is the position. Frequently, pleas of guilty result from bargains made between the accused (or his attorney) and the district attorney. The D.A. may feel that a case is not strong enough to go to a disputed trial. He will therefore propose that if the suspect will plead guilty to a lighter charge, any more serious charges that might be brought will be dropped. Such agreements are often made only shortly before a case is due to come into court. This may mean that the police have had to assemble evidence and witnesses for a full-scale trial. On the other hand, the D.A. may make the bargain before the police have explored the possibility of getting judicially acceptable proof on the major charge. In some jurisdictions, there is an assumption that plea-bargaining will always be a preliminary to appearance before a judge; in Detroit there is a "bargaining prosecutor" permanently stationed outside the criminal courts to haggle with defense attorneys.[6]

This widespread practice has two important consequences for the police. First, it means that they can never be sure which of their cases will be litigated to the full. Thus, they must keep a high standard of records in all cases that *might* reach full trial. Second, it sometimes causes them to prepare a case completely for trial, only to find that a guilty plea has short-circuited the legal system and their efforts will never be tested in court. This does not mean that police efforts have been in vain. Their preparations have probably put the prosecutor in a strong bargaining position, because the defense knows that he *can* go to trial if no agreement is reached, and most defendants will seek a compromise rather than face that.

THE DISTRICT ATTORNEY

Normally, as has been noted, the determination of whether a prosecution is justified is made by a district attorney. He will consider the available evidence and then decide whether to go to trial. The police may be influential in that determination, because they are the filters through which the district attorney receives his information.

There are many matters that a prosecuting lawyer must consider, apart from rules of evidence and questions of prosecution policy. One is whether the police officers involved in the case will present their testimony effectively. Today, many cases revolve essentially around the question: "Does the court believe the police officer or not?" There is no matter of law involved. If things happened as the officer says they did, then the accused must be found guilty. On the other hand, if the court distrusts the officer's version of the facts, an acquittal will result. Naturally, it is a common tactic of defense counsel to seek to discredit police testimony by showing that it is untruthful, or at least mistaken.

A district attorney knows this very well. He will therefore beware of any case in which he thinks the police have "stretched a point." It is humiliating for the D.A.'s office, as well as for the police officers concerned, if a prosecution is dismissed because police evidence has been disbelieved.

There are three ways in which a case may come to a district attorney's notice. First, a member of the public may complain directly to him. If he is an elected D.A., he is probably going to pay rather more attention to such a complaint than would one who is appointed. Second, an official or semiofficial group may make a complaint. Such groups range from federal or municipal agencies to private vigilante groups. Third, he will receive cases from his local police department. This third category of referral will account for the huge majority.

In dealing with cases that come into his office, a D.A.'s legal responsibility is straightforward. He must first decide, on the basis of facts before him, whether any criminal offense has been committed. Most of the files sent to him by the police will pose no problem to him in this respect; the police know the substantive law pretty well and only rarely will legal technicalities relating to the charges prevent prosecution. But in the cases that members of the public or semiofficial groups refer to him, a D.A. may find that no offense has been shown, even assuming that all the facts complained of are true.

If this initial hurdle has been passed, a D.A. must then consider whether adequate proof is available for prosecution. Here, highly technical questions may arise. There may be rules of evidence that impose a particularly heavy burden of proof upon the prosecution. An example of such a rule is that *corroboration* must be produced if a rape prosecution is to succeed.[7] There are also rules of evidence that exclude proof because it has been wrongfully obtained; for example, a coerced confession is not admissible against an accused.[8]

Even if a case can clearly be made out and there is ample evidence to go to trial, a public prosecutor may nevertheless not prosecute. Here, practical considerations may override legal ones.

REASONS FOR NOT PROSECUTING

A district attorney may decide not to prosecute a case because he simply does not have the staff available for it. Many D.A.s' offices are short of lawyers and do not have the money to hire more. In this respect, state prosecutors may fail to prosecute for the same reasons that police departments fail to investigate; they are already over-extended.

Another allied problem is that assistants in D.A.s' offices are frequently inexperienced and straight out of law school. They are therefore less effective in court than they might be. This use of prosecuting offices as a training ground for lawyers was severely criticized thirty years ago, with the observation "one cannot but wonder how it is that anyone is convicted of crime when the work of the prosecutor's office is conducted by those who are merely learning how to try lawsuits." [9] Nevertheless, a generation later it remains true that much prosecution work is done by inexperienced counsel; in 1968, an ex-Assistant United States Attorney recounted glee-fully how a young prosecutor had to "fake it" because of his inexperience in a probable cause hearing.[10]

When problems do not arise in the D.A.'s office, they may arise because court facilities are inadequate. In many jurisdictions, there are substantial backlogs of criminal cases. In 1968, for example, there were 6,100 pending criminal trials in Philadelphia; in New York City the figure was 3,811. In spite of the guarantee to each citizen in the United States Constitution of a "speedy trial," this is a practical impossibil-ity in big cities. A district attorney in a city will do all he can to stop adding to his backlog and to avoid instituting addi-tional prosecutions.

Furthermore, a huge amount of money is invested in any criminal trial. The bulk of it is paid by the taxpayer. While it is true that unless an accused is indigent he will have to pay for his own counsel, the courtroom facilities, the legal ex-penses of prosecution, the heavy expenditure upon detection and assembling judicially acceptable proof will all be paid out of public funds. Public prosecutors often consider ex-pense in deciding whether to prosecute. It may be inexpen-sive to prosecute a rape; it is quite expensive to try any kind of fraud. District attorneys, especially elected ones, are con-cerned with "results," which means in their parlance getting a high percentage of convictions in the cases they prosecute. Where the expense of prosecution is high, they may well decide not to bother. There are many types of crimes about which little public indignation exists, which a D.A. can safely forbear from prosecuting.

THE INFLUENCE OF THE POLICE

In theory, the decision to prosecute lies with the district attorney, but the vast majority of cases come to him from the police and before he ever sees the papers in a case, the police have made some important decisions. They have already decided that their file on the matter is worth forwarding to the D.A.; they will also have decided how worthy of intensive investigation a particular case is. Broadly, if a case has not been probed to any great extent, it is unlikely to reach trial. The police therefore influence the nature of cases that finally reach court because they control the flow of information to the public prosecutor. To some extent, he sees the files sent from the police department through the eyes of the police. They are his source of information. (Some district attorneys' offices hire private investigators directly, thereby by-passing the police department. The D.A.'s office for the borough of Manhattan in New York City is an example of this.[11] This procedure is unusual, and generally the special investigator deals with only a small proportion of particularly "sensitive" cases.)

In many jurisdictions, the public prosecutor has some power to order police investigations himself, but this is not such an awesome strength as might be supposed. It is rare that a prosecutor wishes to deploy police resources in radically different ways from those chosen by the police department. Besides, an investigation ordered by the D.A. is still conducted by the same police department and hence the information he receives will go through the same filter. Thus, the police can substantially influence the decision to prosecute by the emphasis they choose to give to particular cases considered by the district attorney.

Here again, we see the failure of the law to adjust to the growth of professional police forces. The discretion of the police greatly influences the public prosecutor. There have been recent suggestions that police discretion should be exercised according to "guidelines." Yet even with these we see that law will play a subordinate role. "Guidelines" are not legal rules.

THE LAW'S DELAYS

The backlog of criminal cases in many areas is self-perpetuating; the longer the list of pending trials, the more likely it is that things will go wrong. A crucial piece of evidence may be lost in one case, thereby preventing prosecution. A witness may die in another case. An effective prosecution is impossible where documents, reports, and real evidence are missing. Yet the longer the time before a case comes to trial, the greater the danger that material will be lost.

Delay in the trial list makes it essential that police records be kept carefully. Record-keeping is the responsibility of the police department as a whole, and there is only a limited amount an individual officer can do. Nevertheless, he can aid the department in two ways. First, he can ensure that any report he submits is clearly marked with a case number and the name of the accused, or the suspect. Second, he can retain either a carbon copy or photostat of any report he submits. If records are lost, he will still have substitute material at hand. If he signs the copy reports (which he retains) at the time of writing, they may qualify for admission into evidence at trial.

In some police departments there are rules preventing an officer from removing his reports from files because the information contained in them is confidential. Such rules, however, usually do not prohibit an officer from retaining copies in his station house desk or locker. If there is any doubt about the matter, an officer should ask his superior whether he may.

Police notebooks are generally retained by the officer who compiled them. They are often extremely valuable in the courtroom, because the law allows a witness to "refresh his memory" from such materials if they were written at the time of the events they describe. They should never be destroyed, no matter how useless they appear. No one can predict what their ultimate significance may be. In addition, an officer who destroys notes may lay himself open to a charge by the defense that he destroyed them because they contained information favorable to the accused. One defense counsel tried to impeach the whole of an officer's testimony because it was known that he had destroyed notes of an interview with two persons who later became prosecution witnesses.[12] Luckily, this defense did not succeed, because the court found that the officer destroyed them only because he believed they were valueless. But if the officer had retained a copy of his notes, that ground of appeal could never have been raised.

The danger that police records may be lost is particularly great when there is a waiting list of cases for trial. A policeman who saves his records is serving justice. Furthermore, the weight given to any oral testimony he may offer in court often depends upon the backing of his prior statements in police records.

THE PRESSURE OF TIME

Most defense lawyers preparing a case for trial spend much time interviewing and coaching their witnesses. Admittedly, the dividing line between interviewing witnesses and handing them a script is a vague one. Nevertheless, the practice is common among trial lawyers.

Such attention is rarely given to witnesses for the prosecution. As has been explained, district attorneys' offices are frequently overloaded with work. Their lawyers cannot devote much time to interviewing witnesses. It is usually assumed that a policeman needs no help in giving his evidence, and even if other witnesses are given pre-trial aid, policemen are not. The result is that an officer has had less time devoted to him before trial than any other witness for the prosecution or defense. Frequently, he has only a small idea of the relative importance of the facts to which he will testify, and he is therefore vulnerable to the tactics of opposition counsel.

A typical situation was uncovered in the District of Columbia:

Successful prosecution is . . . heavily dependent upon efficient police investigation and trial preparation. Nevertheless, liaison between the police and the United States Attorney's office has been inadequate. Few new assistants have more than a casual awareness of police procedures, and learn these only coincidentally as they examine individual cases. In turn, the police receive only occasional direction from the United States

Attorney on matters of such prosecutive importance as confessions and search and seizure. Lectures given by assistants provide some instruction in the law, but on the whole are insufficient. Rapport is erratic; policemen attribute lost cases to excessive prosecutorial fastidiousness, and prosecutors blame police carelessness.[13]

The assumption that a police officer can handle himself on the witness stand better than the average layman is probably justified. The police do know more than the ordinary citizen about courts. Nevertheless, in the absence of careful preparation by the D.A.'s office, nearly every policeman can benefit from a deeper understanding of procedure and evidence in court. It has been suggested by the President's commission on crime that some police departments would benefit from having their own legal advisers, independent of the public prosecutor. One of the functions of such an adviser would be to prepare policemen for the courtroom.[14] Whatever the merits of this proposal, it has not been widely implemented; and even if it were, a police officer once on the witness stand would be thrown back on his own resources of knowledge.

DEFENSE TACTICS BEFORE TRIAL

The overworked prosecutor may not have the time to spare for pre-trial interviews, but the defense attorney has. Indeed, he will seek out a police officer who is going to testify for the state. He may display extraordinary friendliness of which a policeman should beware, for a lawyer does not do this without an ulterior motive. That motive is best described in a manual for the guidance of defense counsel:

Generally, the more frequently counsel speaks with the police and prosecutor the better. Every conversation with an individual officer gives the lawyer a little more information about how the officer views the case, what he thinks the evidence is and how anxious he is to see the defendant convicted. Details of what the officer says may be useful in cross-examination later, if the case comes to trial.[15]

In other words, the friendly defense attorney seeks to pump the police officer for information.

An officer faced with this situation should remember that no witness is legally bound to speak with anyone. He may refuse to talk at all about the case if he wishes. If he does that, and the defense attorney is persistent to the point of annoyance, he is possibly breaching professional ethics and can be restrained by a complaint made to his bar association. It must be the personal decision of an officer whether he will talk to defense counsel, but if he does, he should remember that he may be giving the defense ammunition with which to attack the prosecution.

It is important that a policeman understand that he is not obliged to say anything to the defense, because the prosecutor cannot instruct him not to do so. In *Gregory v. United States*, 369 F.2d 185 (D.C.C.A. 1966), at 189, it was held that if a prosecutor tells prosecution witnesses not to speak to the defense, or not to speak to the defense without the prosecutor being present, it amounts to denial of fair trial and a conviction may be reversed as a result. But if a police officer himself chooses not to speak with the defense, that is his right.

The police officer should not believe that defense counsel will help the police in exchange for favors received. The same lawyers' manual quoted above advises defense attorneys: "It is not prudent to tell the police of counsel's plans or the facts he knows or his client's reaction to the charge." [16] In other words, a police officer who talks to the defense almost certainly helps the defendant, but cannot hope that the defense will aid the prosecution.

The officer should remember that his fraternization with defense attorneys also may create a misleading and undesirable impression; many lawyers imply to their clients that they have "influence" with the police, or prosecutor, or judge. They make a point of maintaining ostensibly friendly relations with all such personnel in order to create that impression. The result can be that an officer who is overwilling to talk with defense counsel gets branded as "open to persuasion."

NOTES

[1] *The Challenge of Crime in a Free Society* (New York: Avon Books, 1968), p. 336.

[2] *Ibid.*, p. 381–382.

[3] Edwin M. Borchard, *Convicting the Innocent* (New Haven: Yale University Press, 1932), p. xv.

[4] E.g., Rule 11, Federal Rules of Criminal Procedure.

[5] *Handbook on Criminal Procedure in the United States District Court* (St. Paul, Minn.: West Publishing Co., 1967), p. 84.

[6] Martin Mayer, *The Lawyers* (New York: Dell Publishing Co., 1968), p. 169.

[7] *Black's Law Dictionary*, 4th ed., defines corroboration as "evidence supplementary to that already given and tending to strengthen and confirm it; additional evidence of a different character to the same point." In a rape case, it would corrobo-

rate an absence of consent to intercourse if the complainant's genital regions showed signs of forcible entry, e.g., excessive bruising.

[8] The Supreme Court has held that the term "coercive" should be widely construed in this context; see *Miranda v. Arizona*, 384 U.S. 436 (1966). For a discussion of this and other related cases see Kevin Tierney, "Anglo-American Attitudes to Self-Incrimination" 6 *American Criminal Law Quarterly* 26 (1967).

[9] Albert S. Osborn, *The Mind of the Juror* (Albany, N.Y.: The Boyd Printing Co., 1937), p. 186.

[10] J. Shane Creamer, *The Law of Arrest, Search and Seizure* (Philadelphia: W. B. Saunders Co., 1968), p. 108.

[11] For an account of the functions of such an investigator, see Harold R. Danforth and James D. Horan, *The D.A.'s Man* (New York: Crown Publishing, 1957).

[12] *Miller v. United States*, 169 F.2d 967 (D.C.C.A. 1948), at 968 (abortion).

[13] *President's Commission on Crime in the District of Columbia, Report on the Metropolitan Police Department* (Washington, D.C.: Government Printing Office, 1966), pp. 330–331.

[14] *Ibid.*, p. 32.

[15] Anthony G. Amsterdam, 1 *Trial Manual for the Defense of Criminal Cases* (Philadelphia: ALI-ABA Joint Committee for Continuing Legal Education, 1967), para. 92.

[16] *Ibid.*, para. 95.

5 ★ Appearance and Manner in Court

The appearance and manner of a witness is important in influencing a court. It has even been suggested that the physical appearance of a police officer who is a witness has more bearing upon the outcome of a case than his truthfulness.[1] Even if that statement is overdrawn, it is certain that truth alone does not make a good witness:

> Even with all the truth on his side he may flounder about so badly during cross-examination that his testimony will be counted out.[2]

In deciding upon what is appropriate in appearance and manner, the atmosphere of the particular court must be taken into account. Courts vary widely from extreme formality to informality. A police witness has certain advantages over a lay witness; first, it seems natural for a police officer to be testifying—he is in his element—whereas an ordinary citizen may be completely overawed; second, the problem of appearance is largely solved for him if he appears in uniform.

Nevertheless, it is not easy for any witness to feel comfortable in court; for many persons, a court appearance has the connotation of being thrown to the lions:

There are many reputable, self-respecting persons who all their lives remember with hot indignation their one experience on the witness stand, and many deserving cases are defeated because of the absence of important witnesses who under no conditions can be induced to testify because of their terror of cross-examination. By almost any means they will avoid being called as witnesses.[3]

This fear may be greater in those who have not acted as witnesses than in those who have. In practice, giving testimony is not the ordeal that television shows might lead the public to believe. Every week the star cross-examiner reduces a witness to pulp on television; in reality, that is rare.

This chapter discusses both the appearance of a police officer as it should be on the witness stand and the manner in which his testimony should be given.

WEARING A UNIFORM

Generally, a police officer should testify in his uniform, though practice varies in some courts. For example, in Connecticut "In superior court it is preferred that the officer wear civilian clothes unless he is called in suddenly from his patrol or beat."[4] There are arguments that may be put forward against wearing a uniform on principle—one text suggests that it is an illegitimate attempt to impress the court[5] —but it is difficult to see why the court should be specially impressed. Clearly, few judges have felt there is any merit in this point, because there are no jurisdictions which actually prohibit a policeman from appearing in uniform.

However, a witness is entitled to wear a uniform on the stand only if he would wear it officially off the stand. Thus officers who perform their duties in plain clothes should appear in court in plain clothes. The simplest guideline for officers in this position is to dress similarly to the lawyers engaged in the case—usually in a plain dark suit.

Occasionally, wearing a uniform on the stand can have legal consequences that affect the outcome of a whole trial. If an officer has left the police force between the date of the alleged offense and the trial, it may be a misrepresentation of his status to wear a uniform. Equally, there are circumstances in which failure to wear a uniform can result in mistrial, as a fascinating English case illustrates:[6]

A man who had been arrested on the night of an annual public celebration sued the arresting officer for false imprisonment and assault. Between the time of the arrest and the plaintiff's action, the defendant officer had been reduced in rank from chief inspector to station sergeant, but this fact was not known to the plaintiff. On the advice of his counsel, the officer appeared during trial in plain clothes, because to have worn his uniform would have revealed his loss of rank. Throughout his testimony, his counsel addressed him as "Mr." and not by his rank of sergeant, and when the plaintiff's counsel referred to him as "chief inspector," the defendant did nothing to correct him.

On appeal, it was held that the defendant's failure to wear a uniform, coupled with the concealment of his loss of rank, had deceived the court on a matter of vital significance relating to the defendant's credibility. The trial verdict in favor of the defendant officer was overturned. The officer had been testifying under false colors.

WEARING GUN AND NIGHTSTICK

In many forces the gun and nightstick comprise part of an officer's uniform. In spite of this, it is best not to wear them in court; they may symbolize oppression and could create unfavorable associations in the minds of judge and jury.

THE ATMOSPHERE OF A COURT

There are great variations in the tone of court proceedings, and these variations will have an influence upon the manner of an officer's testimony. Some courts are hurried, others are leisurely; some are dignified, others are free and easy; some sit with a jury, some with judge alone. The nature of the charges against the accused can affect the atmosphere of the court, too; offenses involving personal violence will create tension more than will property crimes.

There is no barometer of court atmosphere, and an officer must rely on his own judgment to gauge it. But wherever he is in doubt, it is a safe rule to err on the side of formality, which is more palatable in any circumstances than laxity. After all, legal proceedings are a serious matter for the accused, and he has the right to expect that they will be taken seriously. In particular, a witness should never attempt to be humorous on the witness stand; there are, alas, judges and lawyers who do so, but their example should not be followed.[7] A policeman should always show that he treats his job seriously, no matter what the attitude of other participants in a trial may be.

The most important variable in a court's atmosphere is whether a jury is sitting. Where one is not, the proceedings will probably be less formal and more relaxed.

APPEARING BEFORE A JUDGE ALONE

There are many cases when a policeman will testify before a judge sitting without a jury. The major instances are when: (1) the accused has waived his right to jury trial (see Chapter 7, pages 98–99); (2) the right to jury trial does not attach to the particular proceedings, as with certain courts-martial prosecutions; (3) proceedings are held before a judge alone in anticipation of a trial by jury, as with the preliminary hearing and hearings of pre-trial motions in which the prosecution or defense ask that certain evidence be suppressed at trial.

Where there is no jury, there is less need for the lawyers on either side to take aggressive stands, because a judge is unlikely to be influenced by the tricks of the trade. There is usually less oratory where there is no jury; judges are less inclined to be swayed by it. In the absence of a jury, judges tend to take a more dominant role in proceedings and ask more questions of counsel and witnesses alike. The replies that a witness makes, even if they are improper, cannot do the damage that a similar reply before a jury might do. Of course, a witness should not become reckless where there is no jury, but the need for caution is less.

Hearings without a jury do not usually determine the ultimate issue of a defendant's guilt or innocence.[8] Rather, they explore collateral issues. But the fact that guilt is not determined does not mean such proceedings are unimportant. On the contrary, cases are won or lost in pre-trial motion hearings:

> If it is true that law enforcement officers are at war with the criminal to protect the peace of the citizen, then it is certainly true today that most of the decisive legal battles in this war against crime are being fought not at trial, but at the suppression hearing.[9]

Suppression hearings—so called because one side or the other hopes to have evidence suppressed—have a special significance for the officer witness, because they often raise directly the issue of the legitimacy of police conduct. The most important instance is the probable-cause hearing, always held before a judge without a jury, in which police action is scrutinized with great care.

A witness will sense for himself the difference between jury and non-jury proceedings. In the non-jury proceedings, however, he should know what a judge is looking for, so that he can present his testimony in the best possible light.

PROBABLE-CAUSE HEARINGS

Probable-cause hearings are the most important instances of proceedings without a jury in which the police officer testifies. They are held to determine whether the means by which the government procured evidence was legal. If it was not, the prosecution may not profit from the fruits of its illegality, and the evidence will be excluded from the trial. This may result in the prosecution's being dropped, and it is therefore crucial that the D.A. win in the probable-cause proceedings.

The law forces the courts to pay almost as much attention to police conduct as they do to the conduct of defendants. A probable-cause hearing is in essence a review of police action in which the defense lawyer seeks to show that the police were without authority to obtain evidence in the way they did. No matter how valuable the evidence that results from an illegal search, it will not be admitted as prosecution evidence at trial. The law does not allow the police to justify themselves by results. This rule has applied to all states since 1961, when the Supreme Court decided *Mapp v. Ohio*, 367 U.S. 643. The Cleveland police made an illegal search of the home of a Miss Mapp and found obscene material, which she was later convicted of possessing.[10] The Supreme Court held that the illegality of the search prohibited the prosecution from relying upon the evidence seized. This particular case left no doubt that the constitutional guarantee of freedom from unreasonable search and seizure would be enforced in state trials.

In these hearings, the rules of evidence are suspended, and therefore a police witness can make an impression upon the judge by emphasizing all the factors that justified the police action in question.

APPEARING BEFORE A JURY

Where proceedings are held before a jury, more restraint is needed than in non-jury hearings. But the manner of a police officer will affect his impact. He should seek to show his integrity and fairness, and avoid officiousness and self-importance.

INTEGRITY

An officer should convey by his demeanor the utmost moral correctness. He knows that he is honest, but the jury can only infer this from his appearance and manner. This should be deliberate, without being pompous. A policeman should not allow himself to be railroaded into unwise, unthinking answers. No witness is under any duty to respond to questions in a split second; he is entitled to think about his answer. If a question requires careful thought, he should politely ask that he be given time to think. Defense counsel may argue to the jury that the pauses were the result of the witness' uncertainty, but then prosecution counsel is equally entitled to say that they indicated an officer's conscientiousness. It is, anyway, much better to take time in answering than to be discredited by an unthinking answer, blurted out in an effort to keep the pace of questions. A jury will appreciate a genuine effort to give fair and accurate responses.

FAIRNESS

There is always a danger that a policeman's involvement with the prosecution may make him overeager to discredit the accused. He may know that the accused has a long string of convictions, but the jury will not, and therefore has no understanding of the reasons for an officer's hostility. It will appear to them as an unfair bias.

In order to avoid the appearance of "prosecution-mindedness," an officer should freely admit any matter favorable to the accused, and should never show anger if his testimony is attacked by the defense. If he is indignant, the jury may infer that he is more concerned with his reputation than with the truth. Calm, good-humored denial is the appropriate reaction to such suggestions.

OFFICIOUSNESS

A policeman should not seem meddlesome or overly authoritative. An officer should make it clear that he does his duty with as little interference as possible in the private lives of ordinary citizens. This is especially necessary when the charges against the accused relate to obstruction of an officer in the course of his duty. Here, the police are vulnerable to a charge of officiousness.

The line between legitimate official actions and officiousness is inevitably a blurred one, and for that very reason jurors will watch a policeman carefully on the stand to see whether he might inflate his authority to an objectionable size. Thus, his courtroom manner may determine the jury's attitude toward an entire sequence of events involving the police and the public.

SELF-IMPORTANCE

If a policeman seems "too big for his boots," a jury will probably be unwilling to convict anyone on his evidence. Self-importance is closely related to officiousness, and resentment of authority is often as much related to the manner of its exercise as to authority itself. A police officer should have the good sense not to let the status of his important work go to his head. The powers given to a modern police officer can be abused so that police conduct appears as bad as criminal conduct. It is for this reason that some people have come to see criminal defendants as brave crusaders against sinister police authority. The police officer on the stand should be an example of his force, and demonstrate to jury and public alike his concern not to abuse his office.

NOTES

[1] E. W. Williams, *Modern Law Enforcement and Police Science* (Springfield, Ill.: Charles C Thomas, 1967), p. 243.

[2] Charles L. Cusumano, *Laugh at the Lawyer Who Cross-Examines You* (New York: Old Faithful Publishing Co., 1942), p. 7.

[3] Albert S. Osborn, *The Problem of Proof,* 2nd ed. (Newark, N.J.: The Essex Press, 1926), p. 371.

[4] Douglas B. Wright and John F. Reardon, *Connecticut Police and Prosecutors Manual* (Hartford, Conn.: Atlantic Law Book Co., 1959), p. 49.

[5] Floyd N. Heffron, *The Officer in the Courtroom* (Springfield, Ill.: Charles C Thomas, 1955), pp. 51–53.

[6] *Meek v. Fleming* 3 All E.R. 148 (1961).

[7] See Martin Mayer, *The Lawyers* (New York: Dell Publishing Co., 1968), p. 170.

[8] Obviously, cases where the accused has waived his right to jury trial are an exception to this generalization.

[9] J. Shane Creamer, *The Law of Arrest, Search and Seizure* (Philadelphia: W. B. Saunders Co., 1968), p. 89.

[10] Since the *Mapp* case, the Supreme Court has ruled that

any law which purports to make possession of obscene material a crime is unconstitutional—see *Stanley v. Georgia* 394 U.S. 557 (1969). Hence, there would today be an additional reason for overturning Miss Mapp's conviction, apart from that given in the text.

6 ★ Honesty and Discretion in Testimony

Jeremy Bentham described witnesses as "the eyes and ears of justice." The growth of professional police forces since Bentham's time has meant that many of those witnesses upon whom justice relies will be policemen, whose professional standards have a direct relationship to the standard of justice that our courts dispense, for although it is rarely made explicit, our law assumes that most witnesses tell the truth most of the time. If it did otherwise, witnesses would not have such importance in our trial system.

Historically, the police have not always enjoyed the highest reputation for courtroom honesty.[1] Even as late as the 1930s, police perjury was found to exist on a wide scale and was described in the famous work *Our Lawless Police* as "the poisoning of the stream of evidence." [2] We may be thankful that since then police standards have greatly improved, but historic distrust has left its legacy in our law; juries may be warned of the interest the police have in obtaining a conviction, and the obvious implication of such a warning is that a jury should look out for police dishonesty.

Another burden from the past that the police carry is public attitudes that are derived from another era, when there were reasons for suspecting police testimony. Many members of the public have doubts about the integrity of some police forces. So do lawyers: one reports that "most of these witnesses will testify truthfully to nine parts of the case and as to the tenth and vital part which may turn the scale of the trial, they do not hesitate to draw upon their imaginations and stretch a point and sometimes even commit downright perjury." [3] In England, where confidence between police and public is much greater than that generally to be found in the United States, a survey in 1962 revealed that 32 percent of the population believed the police "twisted" the evidence they gave in court. [4] There will always be a proportion of people who prefer to think ill of the police, however exemplary police conduct may be, but at the moment the proportion is apparently far above the irreducible minimum.

What is needed, therefore, is that special care be taken to impart in court a sense of the honesty and tact of police evidence. Honesty is respected by prosecution and defense attorneys alike. Jerry Giesler, the famous lawyer, went out of his way to praise a police witness for his candor in a trial in which he was engaged when he came to write his memoirs. [5] Appearing on the witness stand must be an exercise in public relations for all police officers. Honesty is, of course, a duty; but tact is an art that will bring home to skeptical onlookers the fairness of police testimony.

THE DUTY OF HONESTY AND THE OATH

It is easy to see why the law expects honesty from witnesses; miscarriages of justice can so readily follow from perjury that if untruthful witnesses were common, it would probably be fairer to dispense with testimony altogether. In order to encourage witnesses to be honest, courts have from the earliest times required them to swear an oath to tell the truth. The original purpose of the oath was to bring down the wrath of God on anyone who told lies,[6] but in this more secular age the oath is retained partly in order to impress each witness with the solemnity of his duty and partly because perjury is defined in such a way that any prosecutor must prove that a statement was made under oath if he is to succeed.

Policemen are well acquainted with the oath and sometimes allow its familiarity to breed contempt. A well-known advocate once suggested that the policeman's oath should be changed to read: "I swear by Almighty God that whatever I say will not get me into trouble."[7] Of course, the police should treat their sworn obligations very seriously and tell the truth as witnesses regardless of any personal interests with which it conflicts.

PERJURY

Perjury is defined as the willful taking of a false oath in a judicial proceeding, with regard to a matter material to the issue. It is rarely prosecuted, partly because it is only rarely discovered and partly because of the onerous rules of proof that are applied.[8]

It should be noted that perjury involves *deliberate* untruthfulness, and therefore as long as a witness gives his evidence in good faith he cannot be guilty of perjury. The fear of some conscientious policemen that they may "mistakenly" commit perjury is groundless, because it can only be committed by a witness who knows at the time he swears to something that it is false.

Of course, there are many forms of courtroom dishonesty that fall short of the legal definition of perjury. On the whole, the police are not often accused of out-and-out lying on the witness stand and producing a wholly fictitious story with which to delude the court. Rather, they are criticized for slyly embellishing their evidence. Nevertheless, it is important that an officer consider all possible forms of adulterated testimony that the police are suspected of giving.

The most serious and despicable kind of perjury of which the police are accused is the frame-up, by which an accused is convicted on perjured testimony of an offense he did not commit. Unfortunately, some police forces have in the past resorted to framing unpopular individuals, and the public memory of such regrettable incidents dies hard. When frame-ups have occurred, they have usually involved more than one police officer, because a single policeman can scarcely sustain the burden of proof of a wholly trumped-up charge by himself. This has meant that conspiracy to defeat the ends of justice is involved as well as plain perjury.

Where frame-ups happen, they involve persons whom the police dislike and probably believe to be criminals, but upon whom they cannot obtain enough genuine evidence to justify prosecution. It would be naïve to assume that a police officer could go through his career without knowing that a particular fellow officer is "gunning" for some individual. He should take no part in any attempt to convict on false evidence. On the contrary, his duty is to expose any such plan that comes to his attention.

DISHONESTY FALLING SHORT OF PERJURY

Police testimony is sometimes criticized by those who know the criminal courts for forms of dishonesty that fall short of perjury, but that are nevertheless objectionable. The two most frequently cited types of police dishonesty in this category are the embroidering of testimony and testimony that has become an empty formula for placing guilt on the accused.

"Embroidery" is a technique that some judges and lawyers believe to be common. It involves the alteration of peripheral facts involved in a case in order to strengthen the prosecution. In the last section, we noted that perjury had to be dishonesty relating to "a matter material to the issue." Embroidery adds to testimony facts that are not material, but that nevertheless harm the defendant's case rather than help it. Its most frequent form is known in some police circles as "putting in the verbals." An instance is when a police officer describing the arrest, or subsequent conversation on the way to the station house, imputes to the accused some statement like "I knew my luck would run out." Sometimes, verbals go further and indicate to the jury that the accused has had previous brushes with the law, as with "So you've come to see me again, officer."

No doubt some arrestees do make comments of this kind to policemen, but they appear with such regularity that suspicions arise that they are occasionally introduced into police testimony regardless of whether the accused actually uttered them.

"Formula" testimony is a related grievance. In crimes that are frequently prosecuted, police officers seem sometimes to reduce their testimony to a routine incantation that satisfies the court. This testimony is not deliberately false, but in crimes that are charged on a rote basis, the officers concerned simply get used to repeating the same things. An example is the formula beloved for drunken-driving prosecutions: "the defendant's eyes were glassy, his speech was slurred, his breath smelled of liquor, and he walked unsteadily." All this may be true, but in courts where the almost identical words are applied to twenty different defendants each day, an onlooker might be justified in his doubts.

The allegations of embroidery and formula testimony are both difficult to prove and difficult to rebut, because if a policeman has done his job effectively, his evidence inevitably has a "too good to be true" flavor. The police are truly on the horns of a dilemma in this respect: if their testimony is clumsy or insufficient to make out a case, they are labeled inefficient, while if it is impeccable they are accused of manufacturing it.

SUPPRESSION OF FAVORABLE TRUTH

There are circumstances, both on and off the witness stand, in which hiding an important truth can be as misleading as an outright lie. What an officer fails to say in court may be as important as what he says.

Some reputable defense attorneys allege that a major fault of police testimony is the unwillingness of many policemen to concede any fact that happens to be favorable to an accused. Defense counsel tell stories of having to press police witnesses to get them to admit that from his first encounter with the police the accused has consistently denied all knowledge of the offense. Some policemen wish to concede nothing that is helpful to establish a defendant's innocence.

This form of dishonesty falls well short of lying, but is objectionable because it withholds from the court data that it is entitled to have in reaching a decision. Police officers who feel the temptation to suppress truths favorable to the defense (and it is natural that they will feel the temptation on occasion) should remember that a prosecution is strengthened by the generous and fair-minded concession of something that benefits the accused, if in other respects the prosecution is well-grounded. The court will recognize the good faith of the prosecution and give its witnesses greater credence once they have evidence that they are not dominated by partisan prejudice.

It should be noted that there are certain obligations of disclosure that rest on the *prosecutor*, rather than the police.

WHERE POLICE TESTIMONY IS MOST LIKELY TO BE DISPUTED

The obligation of honesty applies naturally to all trials, but there are cases in which police testimony is particularly likely to be attacked by the defense. Here, a special search of an officer's conscience may be in order. These cases are those solely dependent upon police testimony, and they need special care. Where an independent lay witness supports the police testimony, an attack on police credibility may not help a defendant very much, because a jury will probably reason that a lay witness has no incentive to support unreliable police evidence. It is otherwise where the entire prosecution rests upon the word of policemen. The most frequent examples are traffic offenses detected by a squad car that has stopped a delinquent driver. It is because police testimony is vulnerable here that radar equipment is used to detect speeding and other mechanical devices are used to prove drunkenness. They provide corroboration to police testimony that is difficult to dispute. In the vice and narcotics field, still other examples of clandestine offenses occur which the police have to use ingenuity to detect. The arrestee on a charge of homosexual solicitation has almost no defense except to dispute police testimony.

In such cases, a police witness should consider with special care in advance of trial whether his intended testimony is in any way open to attack.

TRUTH AND DISCRETION

A witness swears to tell "the whole truth," but that does not mean what it appears to mean. If a witness were foolish enough to take that part of the oath literally, he might end up telling the court a great deal of inadmissible material. The whole truth is only as whole as the court wishes it to be. Thus, within the obligation to tell the truth a witness has some discretion. The court cannot and does not insist that every point of relevance known to every witness come before it. Indeed, because the court itself does not question witnesses, but leaves that function to the prosecutor and defense counsel, relevant matter may quite possibly never come to its attention. As we know, a defense attorney may choose not to present evidence that tends to show that his client is insane,[9] though it may be highly relevant. The court has still less control over the answers that witnesses give. The content and manner of delivery of testimony is within the witness' control, and he may be selective in the information he imparts. The discretion that a witness has should be used to the best advantage by policemen, who have the dual privilege of knowing more about a case than the average witness and of appearing in court in the course of their professional duties rather than, as with most people, as an interruption to them.

The remainder of this chapter discusses the use of a witness' discretion and indicates some of the pitfalls to avoid. But it is stressed that these should only be avoided where the officer-witness genuinely has a choice. Many narrowly posed questions give a witness no leeway, and he should not try to create an area of discretion for himself where none exists. If a question invites a simple yes or no answer, that is what should be given. The witness is offered the chance to edit his answer only when he is asked a wide question that raises considerations of debatable relevance. If the use of discretion will do violence to the truth, then an honorable witness has no discretion. Only where a choice exists is it suggested that the considerations set out below apply.

TECHNICAL TERMS

All professions develop their own specialized vocabulary of terms not generally known to the public. They may be shorthand, slang, or proper technical words, but whatever their merit when one is talking with colleagues, they are best avoided on the stand. A jury may feel that an officer whose testimony is spiced with unfamiliar words is trying to "blind with science." His pretensions may annoy a jury so much that it does not give adequate weight to his otherwise important and worthwhile testimony. The danger is particularly strong where a prosecution is brought for an offense around which has developed a whole string of special terms—a narcotics offense, for example.

The use of uncommon words will not only irritate a jury, but it may make testimony incomprehensible. A jury may always ask for explanation of what is going on, but many jurors have not the courage to ask for the meaning of words they do not know. Since communication is the aim of all testimony, technical terms can be self-defeating. Plain words will serve the prosecution much better than any show of jargon.

PRO-POLICE SENTIMENTS

A police officer should not express loyalty to his force or to a fellow officer on the witness stand unless there is some special reason for doing so. Such sentiments, however laudable and sincere, may easily be misconstrued by a jury to mean that an officer will say anything to justify police action. Many a defense lawyer has attempted to argue that police evidence is unreliable because there is a conspiracy of mutual support within a local force. Indeed, there have undoubtedly been occasions when fellow officers have modified their testimony so as to present a united front on behalf of their police department. That is a deplorable practice and unfair to an accused person. It is also a foolish practice, since there is nothing discreditable to a police force if two of its employees who witnessed the same event happen to have an honest disagreement about what took place.

The most glaring example of pro-police sentiment is the officer who contrives to tell the court during the course of his testimony that the police are wonderful, that they work harder than other men, that they are possessed of superhuman skills and judgment and never make a mistake. Most modern policemen know better than to launch into a peroration like this, but occasionally one resorts to it when faced with questions that implicitly criticize police conduct. Nothing but harm can come of these outbursts. However strongly an officer believes in them and however true they may be, they are irrelevant to the issues before a criminal court, and the fact that these opinions are volunteered invites a jury to conclude that the police are self-righteous and indiscriminately convinced of their own truths. A similar inference will be made if an officer, without explicitly voicing his approval of police actions, shows great irritation when they are questioned. A display of irritation or impatience may indicate a witness' attitudes just as clearly as words.

An allied danger is for an officer who is a witness to justify his own conduct by saying "all policemen do it that way." That may be true, but it does not conclusively show that his conduct was proper, and again it may raise the thought in the jury's mind that the police believe anything they do is right.

A display of police solidarity may unwittingly create an adverse impression if more than one officer testifies in the same trial and each pats the other on the back in the course of his testimony. Obviously, when two officers testify in the same trial, they should compare notes and, so far as the truth permits, back each other up. If they compared notes before trial, they should admit it if asked on the stand. It is a common-sense thing to do, and they are entitled to do it. But the jury should not be left feeling that if one policeman swore the moon was cheese, so would the other. A contradiction of testimony between two policemen does not automatically condemn the prosecution to failure, and to make all police witnesses agree for the sake of solidarity is not only dishonest, but in many instances transparently obvious to a jury.

ARGUMENT AND CONTROVERSY

In every community there are some subjects about which most people have a strong opinion. These subjects are often political and social controversies, such as race, corruption in public officials, police brutality, and capital punishment. This is by no means an exhaustive list, but given by way of example. There are many issues of much more local significance than any of these which can generate a great deal of heat. So far as possible, a witness should avoid these topics. The rule against a witness' expressing an opinion will prevent direct statements, naturally, but an opinion may be communicated by a particular form of answer.

Controversy is prone to divide a jury, and a jury must be united if any prosecution is to succeed. The courtroom is not the place to air controversial views, but if they arise, they should be dealt with in a restrained way. An indiscreet disclosure of a policeman's personal views may open him to cross-examination designed to show bias. For instance, if a defendant is foreign-born and an officer discloses a poor opinion of persons not born in the United States, the defense attorney will almost certainly suggest to the jury that his client has been victimized and that the police officer's testimony has been distorted by his prejudice.

Sometimes counsel will unethically try to goad a witness into argument by expressing disbelief at his evidence. A witness should not allow himself to be provoked into argument by this or any other technique, for the same reason that they should not engage in controversy—it may displease the jury. It is improper for a lawyer to express his personal opinion in his cases, but there are lax courts. The borderline is rather difficult to maintain. Some attorneys repeat the witness' answers on cross-examination in a disbelieving tone that implies that the answer is extremely unlikely to be reliable. If a policeman says that an automobile was going at thirty miles per hour, the cross-examining attorney may echo the response in a tone that would be appropriate for the statement that pigs have wings. A witness should not be drawn into a squabble with counsel, but should merely let his answer stand. The jury will find a lawyer who acts that way irritating, but they will find a witness who argues with him even more irritating. It is worth ignoring the taunting of a defense lawyer in order to win the jury.

NOTES

* [1] See quotation from Earl Rogers, the nineteenth-century trial lawyer, in Chapter 7, p. 87.

[2] Ernest Jerome Hopkins, *Our Lawless Police* (New York: The Viking Press, 1931), p. 278.

[3] Jules H. Baer and Simon Balicer, *Cross-Examination and*

Summation, 2nd ed. (New York: Fallon Law Book Company, 1948), p. 89.

[4] *The Royal Commission on the Police,* quoted in Richard DuCann, "Police Evidence" 6 *The Lawyer* No. 1 (1963), at 7. As Mr. DuCann observes, the response of the British public had special significance because the question asked in the survey was in no sense a loaded one.

[5] Jerry Giesler, *Hollywood Lawyer* (New York: Pocket Books, 1962), p. 91.

[6] Under the heading "oath," *Black's Law Dictionary,* 4th ed., gives several authorities for the religious purpose of oaths in invoking God's wrath.

[7] Richard DuCann, "Police Evidence," 6 *The Lawyer* No. 1 (1963), at 10.

[8] This is not a problem confined to American courts. In a recent English work on the police it is stated that: "There are far too few prosecutions for perjury in our courts, despite the difficulties involved." Ben Whitaker, *The Police* (London: Eyre & Spottiswoode, 1964), p. 178.

[9] Jack Altman and Marvin Ziporyn, *Born to Raise Hell* (New York: Grove Press, 1968), p. 227.

7 ★ Testimony and the Jury

Traditionally, a jury has been composed of twelve jurors, but there is no magic in this number; for example, there is nothing to prevent a state from using juries of only eight members.[1] Whatever the number of jurors, they must all agree on their verdict. There is no such thing as a "majority verdict" in a criminal trial. This means that the prosecution has to convince every one of the jurors of the guilt of the accused. In this respect, America clings to the common law tradition although the mother-country of the common law does not. England permits majority verdicts of 10 to 2.

An interesting question that has never been decided arises with regard to juries of fewer than twelve. How small may a jury be, while still satisfying the due process and fair trial standards of the Fourteenth Amendment? Obviously, the fewer people there are on a jury, the less formidable the requirement of unanimity becomes. Eight we know to be sufficient. Would six do? Or five, or four?

The major importance of the unanimity requirement is that it gives substance to the burden of proving the defendant guilty "beyond reasonable doubt." The prosecutor must vanquish reasonable doubt from the minds of twelve people if he is to convict. Only one need be doubtful and the prosecution fails. True, there may not be an acquittal, but merely a "hung" jury. Most lawyers, whether for the prosecution or defense, dislike hung juries. They are a nuisance to both sides, because they leave uncertain the very question that the jury was empaneled to decide.

A police officer should realize that it is a considerable achievement to persuade twelve people to agree on a major issue, such as the guilt or innocence of a defendant. Regardless of how strong he feels a case may be, he must recognize that there is never a case in which the prosecution can afford not to put on its best show. A police officer who is a witness is part of that show, and perhaps its star.

We assume that witnesses are essential in a trial. We forget that in former times cases were heard without witnesses. "Trial by ordeal" was common in the Middle Ages. A person accused of crime was made to submit to physical ordeal by the court, and if he survived, he was presumed innocent. If he did not survive, the presumption was that he was guilty and it was God's judgment that he should die. Some of the ordeals were frightful by modern standards—walking over hot coals or being held under water for five minutes were typical. No one gave evidence at such trials.

Since then, our standards of justice have advanced. We no longer believe that Divine wishes are revealed in trial by ordeal. We insist upon secular, rational proofs before we condemn a man. Yet even an insistence upon reason need not require that witnesses appear before the court. Those who have matters of value to lay before the court could put them in writing and never go near the courthouse. Why in fact does American law insist (except in rare instances) that witnesses appear in court?

There are two reasons, both basic to the American conception of law. We believe in the right of an accused person to confront the witnesses against him, and in his right to trial by jury.

THE RIGHT OF CONFRONTATION

An accused person is entitled to hear the evidence against him, and within certain limits, to attempt to undermine it. American law does not stop short at producing witnesses and allowing them to make a speech. A witness cannot simply *denounce* the accused and then walk off the witness stand. He may only testify in response to questions put by counsel (whether for the prosecution or defense) and occasionally by the judge.

The right of confrontation makes it essential that witnesses appear personally before the court. Some jurisdictions allow no exceptions to this rule, but others, including the federal, allow the taking of *depositions.* Depositions are written records of what a witness has said outside the court and they are normally taken when it is impossible for a witness to attend court, because of illness or other good cause.

Where the prosecution seeks depositions from its witnesses, the defendant and his counsel always have a right to attend and cross-examine.

On the whole, the use of depositions is kept to a minimum, because it is far better to produce a witness in court. The testimony, if valuable, will probably have far less effect upon the jury if it is read to them than if it had been given directly before them. Furthermore, tricky disputes can sometimes arise about the limits of examination and cross-examination when a deposition is being taken. Since the process of questioning is basic to the right of confrontation, all ambiguity should be avoided.

The question-and-answer method is one that prevents any witness, whether he be policeman or ordinary citizen, from giving full vent to his opinions. In many instances, it allows a witness to tell only a little of what he knows. There must be thousands of people who have acted as witnesses who have left the court thinking: "If only I had been asked . . ."

By the time a case reaches trial, the police officers involved have a great deal of time, energy, and emotion invested in it. Thus, when they approach the witness stand, they have a great deal of information to impart. The law prevents them from stating all they know and prefers to pick their brains as it chooses. A policeman should not resent this method. His professional experience will tell him how prejudiced and inaccurate a statement can be, even if it is made in good faith. He knows that there are people who will phone the station house with completely false and malicious complaints. He knows that police informants acting in the utmost good faith often turn out to be wrong.

Policemen are not entitled to any special privilege by virtue of their profession. They appear as witnesses on the same basis as anyone else. It may be asked: What can a witness do if he is not asked the "right" questions? The answer is that he can do nothing. He must grin and bear it. He can have no idea of the total strategy that prosecution or defense counsel have mapped out—they do not customarily disclose it. His concern is not the conduct of the case, but merely to do his utmost to answer in a forthright and honest manner questions put to him.

The importance attached to the right of confrontation is

graphically illustrated by a significant New York State decision. A witness for the People gave her evidence-in-chief and then went into convulsions before the defense had the chance to cross-examine her. Defense counsel asked that her direct evidence be struck out, or alternatively that the trial be adjourned until she recovered, but the judge refused and the trial proceeded to conviction. On appeal, the conviction was quashed on the ground that the defendant's right of confrontation had been denied.[2]

The right of confrontation takes on a special importance in a jury trial, because from the impressions that the jury gains of witnesses its verdict will form. In essence, a good witness is therefore one who impresses a jury favorably.

WHAT JURY TRIAL MEANS

Juries are used in nearly all trials of serious offenses. The Supreme Court has recently extended the right to trial by jury to a great many cases that it was thought were not covered by the constitutional guarantee of due process contained in the Fourteenth Amendment. In *Duncan v. Louisiana*, 391 U.S. 145 (1968), the Court held that the right to trial by jury attaches to all state prosecutions that would be entitled to jury trial were they tried in a federal court. This means that many states will be holding more jury trials than ever before. At the time of writing, it is unclear how far-reaching the Supreme Court's decision will be. In New York it has already caused conflicting decisions to be handed down.[3]

Jury trial puts factual questions into amateur hands. Jurors have no special education for their job; they are ordinary citizens who have been called to serve. They return their verdict after being instructed upon the law by the judge, but all extra-legal questions are decided by them. Further, since there is no way of telling whether the jury has heeded the judge's direction on the law, the jury has a great deal of power. It is not easy to upset a jury verdict upon appeal. Hence, the lawyers' axiom, "If you win the jury, you win the case," has meaning for a policeman who is a witness.

It has traditionally been considered a benefit to the accused that he is tried by jury. It has been assumed generally that citizens are more sympathetic to accused persons and less willing to convict than professional judges who sit alone. Recent research has cast some doubt upon this opinion, because the factors that influence a jury are a great deal more complicated than we fully understand. We may say with confidence, however, that it is not inevitably true that juries lean in favor of the defense, for the reason discussed on pages 98–99.

The jury is the most important audience a police officer has when he gives evidence. Consequently, it is important to know what kinds of people serve on juries.

THE COMPOSITION OF THE JURY PANEL

The selection procedures used to choose a jury panel differ widely in the various states. On the whole, jurors are likely to be middle-aged, middle-brow, and middle class. Jurors are more likely to be conventional than not. There are many reasons for this, most of which are outside the scope of this book, but one of them has some interest.

Some lists of prospective jurors are drawn up from recommendations made by various civic organizations. The clerk of the court acts as a censor and decides which organizations are "suitable" recommending agencies. Some of the organizations that are not found suitable are perfectly lawful, but have unconventional purposes. This can happen in selecting federal jurors as well as those who serve in state courts. In New Jersey, district court jurors may be nominated by the Red Cross, but not by nudist camps.[4]

The selection of citizens whose names go onto the jury panel is not the only selection that determines the composition of a jury. There is a further process of selection which is conducted by lawyers engaged in a trial before it starts. This is known as *voir dire*.

THE *VOIR DIRE*

When a court is in session, it calls more persons to serve on the jury than it is going to need. The reason is that either prosecution or defense may object to some of the people called. They have the right to do this either peremptorily or for cause. Peremptory challenges of jurors are those that may be made without giving a reason. Both sides in a trial have the right to such challenges up to a certain number, which varies from jurisdiction to jurisdiction. Usually the number is fewer than ten. Any challenges that either side wishes to make above that number must be for cause, i.e., a reason must be given.

However, the number of peremptory challenges varies according to the charge in some jurisdictions. Furthermore, when there is to be a trial for more than one crime, it is possible to claim peremptory challenges for each crime indicted. These two factors may spectacularly multiply the number of challenges allowed. In the trial of Richard Speck, the murderer of eight nurses in Chicago in 1966, his defense counsel obtained 160 peremptory challenges; Illinois law permits 20 challenges in a murder trial, and for this purpose each murder was treated separately.[5]

What sort of reasons are accepted? Again, this depends upon the law of the particular state in which the proceedings are held, but three important categories of reason are nearly always found. They are disqualification, interest, and bias. A disqualified juror is one who should never have been put on the jury panel at all. An interested juror is one who stands to gain or lose by the outcome of the proceedings, or who is related to one of the parties in some way. The accused's mother would not be qualified to sit on the jury trying her son. The most important type of challenge from a police officer's standpoint is challenge for bias.

In cases that have particularly aroused public interest, it is sometimes a lengthy process to try to find sufficient prospective jurors who have not already formed an opinion about the accused's guilt. In the turn-of-the-century trial of Patrick Calhoun in California, it took three months to pick a jury, during which time 2,371 prospective jurors had been found to be biased.[6]

In many courts, counsel for the accused is permitted to ask each person presented for jury duty questions designed to show bias or prejudice that would prevent him from giving a "true verdict according to the evidence." An obvious example would be an attempt to show that a blue-collar juror who might sit in a case in which the accused was a rich businessman had class prejudice. Most crucially, from our point of view, a defense attorney is allowed to ask questions relating to a prospective juror's attitude toward police testimony. One textbook for defense attorneys recommends that would-be jurors be asked whether they know any members of the police force.[7] A frequently asked question on *voir dire* is: "Are you inclined to give more weight to the testimony of a police officer merely because he is a police officer than to any other witness in the case?"[8] This is a permissible inquiry in many criminal cases because the evidence against the defendant will come mainly, if not exclusively, from police officers. If the answer given was "yes," the prospective juror would be dismissed for cause, because his inclination to believe a policeman more than anyone else would make his verdict unfair.

Whether or not to allow such questions is within the discretion of the judge, who will consider just how important police testimony is going to be in the forthcoming trial. If police evidence is going to be of major importance, he must allow such questions, otherwise any conviction that is obtained can be reversed on appeal. Whether police testimony is crucial depends on the particular facts. It will be crucial when the prosecution relies exclusively on police evidence, or when a single officer's testimony is "virtually the entire case for the prosecution."[9] On the other hand, when only one officer will testify and there will be thirteen other witnesses for the state, the judge is entitled to prevent counsel from asking prospective jurors such a question.[10] In some cases of seriousness, the question is permitted by the court in order to give the defense no ground for later complaint, even though police testimony is not crucial.

The principle behind all this is a common-sense one: legally, all witnesses are equal. A police officer is entitled to credence as much or as little as any other witness; a jury may not assume that one class of witnesses is inherently more truthful than any other or that a particular group never tells the truth. For example, it is wrong for a jury to assume that priests are more truthful than garbage men. If a judge instructed a jury that it should prefer the testimony of a priest to that of a garbage man, because priests are more reliable than garbage men, he would be committing a serious error of law. The jury would be entitled in such a case to prefer the garbage man's evidence to the priest's.

This does not mean, of course, that jurors do not make distinctions between different kinds of witnesses. They probably do—but if they declare openly that they believe policemen more readily than others, they will not serve on a jury. One of the objections to the entire *voir dire* procedure is that it discloses bias only in those prospective jurors who are naïve enough to admit their prejudice. However, it is a well-entrenched system and will not be abolished in the near future.

As a result of *voir dire*, a policeman knows that if his testimony is crucial to the prosecution, the jury has been chosen because its members have sworn they will *not* give special weight to what he says just because he is a policeman. Therefore, the personal and individual impression that an officer makes is of the utmost importance.

In most jurisdictions, *voir dire* is conducted by counsel, but there are some in which it is done by the judge. This is the method in federal criminal courts. In such jurisdictions, the attorneys for the two sides submit the questions they wish to have asked beforehand, and the judge accepts those he thinks are permissible..

The *voir dire* process is open to criticism; as has been

pointed out, questioning members of the jury panel is a very unreliable way of eliciting prejudice. A juror who conceals his prejudice while being questioned is unlikely to be discovered. Furthermore, the whole basis upon which lawyers and judges assess jurors is highly subjective. The judge who conducted the Sheppard murder trial in Ohio in 1954 described the jury as "a fair and impartial group of people" and went on:

> I doubt if under any conditions at any time anywhere in this state you could get a better-looking group of people and a more intelligent group of people . . . who can properly try this case under the guidance of the court. . . .

In fact, the jury that the judge so optimistically and confidently appraised from its appearance had a member who was a convicted sex offender who could not properly try the case. This was discovered only after trial began.[11]

THE RESPONSE OF A JURY

A policeman cannot hope that his appearance will evoke an entirely neutral response from a jury. Some jurors will respect the police and for them a policeman symbolizes law and order. To others, the police may have associations with oppression. Most people probably have ambivalent attitudes toward the police; a policeman is an authority-figure, and like other such figures, he may be resented at one stage, yet turned to for help at another.

Prejudice against the police as witnesses has a long history. A great nineteenth-century defense attorney formed this opinion:

The average man on any jury does not, will not, believe anything a policeman says in court. No brighter, if as bright, as
the man in the street, nevertheless the policeman is a trained
observer. Ninety-nine times out a hundred, he is more accurate
at describing any fast-moving event, such as a murder, a
shooting, an accident, than any layman. Automatically, he has
been conditioned to know time, to watch people, to take in a
whole scene and to remember details. Just the same, you cannot convict the lowest criminal on the sole word of a policeman. At once, the jury assumes the cop is prejudiced.[12]

Things are not as hopeless as that now, but every policeman
should be aware that such attitudes linger on.

An officer cannot hope to alter individual jurors' stereo-
types of the police, but he can aim to bring favorable associations and impressions to the fore. Any witness has influence
upon a jury according to the impression he makes. A conviction can result only if every juror agrees upon the guilt of an
accused, whereas an acquittal does not need unanimity.
Above all, a policeman wishes his testimony to be believed.
The impressions he must give are of integrity and fairness;
the impressions he must avoid are of self-importance and
officiousness, which have been discussed in Chapter 5, pages
57-60.

HOW QUESTIONS SHOULD BE ANSWERED AND
HOW COURTS DEAL WITH IMPROPER ANSWERS

An elementary rule in facing courtroom questions is to
answer briefly and to the point. A jury is quick to recognize
when a witness is trying to say more than he is entitled to
say. With an ordinary citizen, a jury may take a sympathetic

view, but it is less inclined to do so with a policeman, because it will feel a policeman ought to know better. Prolonged answers may convey to the jury that a police witness is saying more than he is entitled to do. No jury will respect that.

Improper answers will almost certainly incur the judge's displeasure. A police officer should always seek to avoid that, because a judge may give instructions to the jury which warn it that police testimony may not be wholly reliable. But apart from such a danger, a police officer should be aware that courts have three courses open to them to deal with improper responses from a witness.

First, a witness can be cited in contempt of court. This means that his impropriety has been so great that it amounts to disrespect of the court. Normally, a court hesitates to hold a witness in contempt. On the other hand, a police officer may be assumed to have more experience and knowledge of courts than ordinary citizens, and therefore higher standards may be expected of him. Punishment may be imprisonment, or fine, or both and in some jurisdictions a judge is entitled to deal with a contemptuous witness on the spot.

Second, a judge may simply tell the jury to ignore a witness's objectionable words. This is a frequent method of dealing with such improprieties. However, a policeman should know that any such statement will appear in the transcript of the trial. That means that it is potentially a ground for appeal. Although a jury has been instructed to ignore inadmissible remarks, the defense may always claim that the effect of the words was so great that no jury could truly have ignored them (see pages 95–96).

Third, a judge may ignore improper statements completely. If he does so, it is not because he thinks the words acceptable, but because he does not wish to draw further attention to them. He may believe that justice is better served by letting inadmissible remarks pass without comment than by giving a formal instruction to ignore them.

When a judge takes the last course, he is making assumptions about jury psychology that have not been, and by their nature cannot be, proven. He is assuming that some matters in the courtroom pass over the jurymen's heads. Whether this is so, no one knows. The practice is dangerous, because although the judge passes such inadmissible material, it can still be a ground for appeal in many jurisdictions.

A conscientious officer will avoid objectionable statements on the witness stand. However, there are always occasions when he cannot know how far his answers should go. As often as not, this is the fault of the lawyers conducting the case, whose questions may have been broad, or irrelevant, or vague. In such circumstances, no officer can be blamed if the court finally rules his answer should be struck out. Provided he answers in good faith, he will not be held in contempt. If the jury is instructed to ignore an answer he has made, he should apologize politely. It is enough to say "I'm sorry, your honor, I didn't know how far I should go." By doing so, he emphasizes his good faith to judge and jury alike.

REFUSAL OF A WITNESS
TO ANSWER QUESTIONS

May a witness refuse to answer questions? One way of avoiding improper answers is, after all, not to answer.

Any witness may plead the Fifth Amendment, which provides that a witness may not be compelled in any criminal action "to be a witness against himself." However, it would be unusual for a policeman to hide behind the amendment, because it implies that he has committed a criminal offense. One police text takes the position that a policeman should be dismissed if he pleads the Fifth Amendment.[13]

However, since that was written, the Supreme Court has considered the position of a police officer who pleads the Fifth Amendment. In *Garrity v. New Jersey*, 385 U.S. 493 (1967), it held that a police officer may not be offered the choice between incriminating himself or losing his job. In other words, a policeman may plead the Fifth Amendment and still retain his livelihood. In spite of *Garrity*, one cannot see how a policeman could hide behind the privilege against self-incrimination without some damage to his career. His reputation must suffer and his superiors must surely take it into account when considering his rank and responsibilities.

Unless a witness refuses to answer on the ground of the Fifth Amendment, he must answer questions put to him, and his failure to do so can be punished by the court. Usually, such punishment is imposed because refusal to answer amounts to a contempt of court. But in some jurisdictions a witness' refusal to answer is a separate criminal offense, for which a prosecution may be instituted.[14]

A police officer places his career in jeopardy if he pleads the Fifth Amendment, and it is difficult to envisage any circumstances in which he would be justified in refusing to answer a question properly put to him. On the other hand, a prosecution will be greatly aided if the police warn the D.A. in advance that a prosecution witness might plead the Fifth Amendment.

It should be noted that an *accused* may always avoid an-

swering questions by choosing not to testify on his own behalf. This is discussed in Chapter 8, pages 106–107.

INSTRUCTIONS TO JURIES REGARDING
THE TESTIMONY OF THE POLICE

At the end of a trial, a defense attorney is entitled to request the judge to instruct the jury upon matters of evidence. A defense attorney may ask that the judge instruct
that police testimony may be suspect because of "the natural
bias of police officers." The judge may so instruct: "If the
trial judge feels that it is necessary, he may give the instruction. If he does not feel it is proper under the circumstances
he need not. The decision upon the matter is based upon his
sound discretion." [15]

The risk that such a caution may be issued to a jury should
emphasize how important it is that a police officer should
appear fair and honest on the witness stand. By doing so, he
ensures that a judge will not give this jury instruction.

This jury instruction highlights the ambiguous position of
the police in our legal system, as noted in Chapter 1. Although a police officer testifies on the same basis as any citizen, and the law does not recognize police forces as a separate entity to which special rules apply, the jury instruction
refers to the "natural bias" of policemen generally.

SOME INDICATIONS OF JURY ATTITUDES

It is notoriously difficult to acquire reliable information
about how juries work. One of the reasons for this is the

legal rule that jury deliberations are secret. Not only does it amount to contempt of court to question jurors about how they arrive at their decisions, but the American Bar Association holds it to be unethical for lawyers to do so.[16] The consequence is that we remain largely ignorant of one of our major legal devices. This has been a constant source of frustration to trial lawyers, who wish to know what most easily persuades a jury. Percy Foreman, the Texas criminal defense lawyer, used to spend long hours in a men's room adjoining the juryroom at his local criminal court, eavesdropping on jury deliberations so that he knew how verdicts were reached.[17]

On pages 86–87 of this chapter, we noted that most jurors have ambivalent attitudes toward the police. There is evidence that juries form particular views about police conduct as it is revealed in the courtroom and that those views can influence verdicts. In a recent study of cases in which police officers were the *victims* of assault during the course of a forcible arrest, it was concluded that "the jury at times shows a special indulgence for the defendant." [18] In one case, a jury acquitted a man who had assaulted the chief of police of a small community; in another case, a man actually killed a policeman and yet was acquitted. In the case involving the police chief, the judge would have convicted if he had been sitting without a jury. The investigators who made the study conclude that these cases indicate "the depth of the jury's sentiments against use of excessive force by the police." [19]

Naturally, we should be careful in drawing conclusions of a general nature from evidence such as this. But it seems clear that the police cannot always rely upon jury sympathy, even when their conduct has been within the strict bounds of the law. In Chapter 10, dealing with the defense of entrapment, we shall come across further evidence that juries are willing to acquit admitted criminals where police misconduct has been shown.

The inference that the police must draw is obvious. When police conduct has been unsavory, the difficulties of conviction are enhanced. In cases where there has been physical violence between a police officer and a member of the public, special care should be devoted to testimony. It should stress that the amount of force used by the police was the minimum required to control the suspect and that the police do all they can to avoid physical violence. A mild, reasonable, and humane demeanor on the stand by all police witnesses will be especially important in such cases.

WHY JURIES?

Most police officers have asked themselves at some time: Why do we have juries at all? It is a good question, to which many lawyers believe there is no good answer. Originally, juries were designed to provide a man with "trial by his peers." This meant that he would be tried by people of the same social class that he came from. Indeed, this was carried to its logical conclusion in England, where noblemen could, until the twentieth century, be tried for certain classes of serious crimes only by other aristocrats. Today in America, jury trial does not guarantee that an accused will be judged by people just like him. A railroad worker cannot insist that he be tried by a jury of railroad workers, any more than a banker can have a jury of twelve bank presidents. However, the jury has come to be, in a very rough-and-ready sense, a cross-section of the community. It is necessary to qualify this statement with the words "rough-and-ready," because curious practices persist in some jurisdictions. In New York, for example, any woman who is called to jury service is automatically excused if she requests it, yet the same privilege is not extended to male jurors.[20] The result in New York, as in many parts of the country, is that juries are predominantly male, even though women constitute a majority of the population.[21] Furthermore, jury selection is a haphazard process, in which, as a distinguished transatlantic commentator put it, "there is no guarantee that members of a particular jury may not be unusually ignorant, credulous, slow-witted, narrow-minded, biased or temperamental." [22]

Juries remain in use in criminal cases for two major reasons. The Sixth Amendment of the Constitution guarantees jury trial, and many criminals (and their defending lawyers) believe that juries are more likely to be lenient than are professional judges sitting alone. There is some evidence that supports this belief. In 3,576 trials, judges were asked whether they agreed with the verdict that juries returned. Whereas juries had acquitted in 30.3 percent of the cases, the judges said they would have acquitted in only 16.7 percent.[23]

The justification for jury trial must ultimately come down to a preference for amateur, rather than professional, verdicts. Perhaps this is a good thing and the administration of justice is thereby democratized. There is no doubt, however, that we pay a high price for jury trial. Most of the complicated rules of evidence are thought necessary because the jury will be unduly influenced if it has certain facts before it, e.g., the previous convictions of the accused. Although we constantly praise the jury, we do not trust it with all the facts. In terms of productivity lost, juries cost America millions of dollars a year. Jurors frequently lose weeks of work by being summoned to a jury panel. This loss is not reimbursed to the juror or his employer.[24]

From a policeman's viewpoint, the jury is important because it is the jury that must be convinced of a suspect's guilt. Yet no one really knows how a jury can be convinced, or what the most effective means of persuasion are, because juries are *ad hoc* bodies whose deliberations are secret. Many a lawyer believes he "understands" juries—a whole body of legal folklore has grown up around juries. Some of it can scarcely be taken seriously; all of it is speculative. The fact that lawyers who are constantly engaged in trial work become convinced of certain beliefs regarding jury psychology is inconclusive because, perhaps luckily, they can never be tested.

At best, therefore, recommendations about what should be done in front of a jury are educated guesses. An officer should remember that there is no fixed, immutable, unchanging institution known as a jury, but merely a series of groupings of twelve citizens, brought together for a limited time and for a particular purpose. They may differ greatly one from the other, and no amount of study can reduce jury trial to an exact science.

MISTRIAL WHERE JURY HEARS INADMISSIBLE EVIDENCE

We have seen, in Chapter 3, that rules of evidence are used to keep certain types of information from the jury's ears. Sometimes, in spite of all precautions, a witness will say something that is inadmissible. The various ways in which a trial judge may deal with this eventuality were explained on pages 87–89.

There are occasions, however, in which a witness discloses so much inadmissible material that the whole trial is ruined and a mistrial is declared. That means that all efforts thus far have been in vain and proceedings have to be started all over again. An example comes from the District of Columbia.[25] In a prosecution for murder, robbery, and assault with a dangerous weapon, a police witness for the prosecution twice referred in cross-examination to another crime with which the accused was charged. The defendant's counsel moved for a mistrial, but the trial judge merely ordered that the policeman's answer be stricken from the record and that the jury disregard it. On appeal, it was held that the instruction to the jury was not enough, and that there had been a mistrial.

The reason for this is plain enough. When a jury has heard prejudicial evidence, it cannot merely put it out of mind. As Mr. Justice Jackson put it, "The naïve assumption that prejudicial effects can be overcome by instructions to the jury . . . all practicing lawyers know to be unmitigated fiction." [26] There are, of course, instances where the law regards an instruction to the jurors to disregard what they have heard as sufficient, depending on how serious the prejudice is thought to be.

Such cases should act as a warning to police officers who are tempted to throw into their testimony material that is inadmissible. They may jeopardize the whole trial. An Oklahoma appeal court addressed itself directly to policemen in such situations:

This type of testimony has often been referred to as an "evidential harpoon" that has been wilfully jabbed into the defendant and then jerked out by an admonition to the jury not to consider the same. This court has never condoned, but often criticized, a witness being intoxicated with eagerness in an all out effort to obtain a conviction . . . Officers must be aware that an overzealous attitude is, in most instances, detrimental to the prosecution and often results in a retrial of the case at considerable expense to the state.[27]

Thus, an officer bears a considerable responsibility when on the stand. It is quite possible that he is in possession of inadmissible evidence which he would really like the jury to know. He should, however, resist the temptation, since it is not his duty and may abort the whole proceedings. Just as he should go into the witness box knowing what he should say, it is desirable that he know what he should not say. Any doubts an officer has should be resolved with the prosecutor before he takes the stand.

INADMISSIBLE STATEMENTS VOLUNTEERED BY POLICE OFFICERS

Police officers should avoid making statements on the witness stand of the following sorts: (1) opinions, (2) hearsay, (3) attacking the character or reputation of the accused, (4) introducing the accused's previous convictions, (5) referring to inadmissible confessions. If such matter is injected into criminal proceedings, it may be grounds for a mistrial. This is especially likely if a police officer introduces such evidence, because courts have used as a reason for reversing a conviction the grounds that a police officer ought to know better, and that because of his status in the community, his testimony must have had special weight with the jury. A rationale of this kind was adopted in *Harris v. Oklahoma*, 204 P.2d 305 (1949), where in a trial for attempted rape, a police officer introduced into his testimony the fact that the accused had told him he had attempted to rape three or four other women. This case, like many others, illustrates that the courts will be especially wary of inadmissible testimony falling from a policeman's lips and that an officer in court should be very careful not to give the defense cause for appeal.[28]

WAIVER OF JURY TRIAL

Although the Federal Constitution guarantees a defendant trial by jury if he wants it, he may not want it. If he does not, he may waive the right unless such waiver is prohibited by the *state* constitution concerned. In both the federal jurisdiction and those states that permit waiver, such as New York, a written notice of waiver signed by the defendant personally is required.[29]

A police officer may wonder why a defendant should ever wish to waive jury trial. Since it is known that juries are in most cases more likely to acquit than judges sitting alone, it appears at first sight that an accused who waives a jury is increasing his chance of conviction. There are cases, however, in which a judge sitting alone may better serve an accused's purpose than a jury. The cases that usually justify waiver of jury trial are those in which there is no factual dispute, but a question of law is relied upon by the defense.

If a jury sees that the defendant did something that was plainly "wrong" (whether it amounts in law to a crime or not), its tendency may be to convict, where a judge will acquit on a legal point.

Where a prospective witness hears that the accused is intending to waive jury trial, he will probably be right in thinking that his evidence is uncontroverted. The defendant knows that he cannot impress a jury and therefore is taking his chance with a judge alone. Although a police officer should not use this knowledge as an excuse for laxity, he may be justified in assuming that he need not prepare his testimony in order to captivate the jury in the way normally desirable.

POLICE OFFICERS AS JURORS

There are obviously good reasons for a defense attorney to prevent police officers from serving on a criminal jury. He will feel, probably with some justification, that policemen as a group are "prosecution-minded." However, there is no overall prohibition against policemen serving on juries, and the practice of states differs widely. In some states (e.g., in Oklahoma and South Carolina), law-enforcement officers are statutorily disqualified from jury service. In others, police officers are *exempted* from jury service by statute, but it has been held that this does not prohibit a policeman from serving as a juror—the choice is his.[30] Some jurisdictions have made it a rule of court that policemen should not sit on juries, while others have permitted peace officers to sit.[31]

In general, it seems better that a policeman not sit upon a jury, even if his state's law permits him to do so. Whether or not he suffers from bias, there is always a suspicion that a policeman will tend to favor the prosecution. As the Missouri Supreme Court asked: "Would anyone say that a defendant, tried by a jury consisting of police officers, was accorded a jury trial as contemplated by our Constitution?" It answered: "It seems incompatible with justice that a defendant who has been apprehended by the police, and against whom police officers are going to testify, should be tried by a jury made up of police officers." [32] There seems no good reason why a policeman should serve on a jury, and several good reasons why he should not. Therefore, a policeman who finds himself summoned for jury service should apply for exemption before the summons date. In that way, no controversy can arise and justice will be seen to be done.

NOTES

[1] *Maxwell v. Dow,* 176 U.S. 581 (1900). (The State of Utah's Constitution permitted trial for robbery by a jury of eight.)

[2] *People v. Cole,* 43 N.Y. 508 (1871).

[3] See Lloyd I. Paperno and Arthur Goldstein, *Criminal Procedure in New York* (Massapequa, N. Y.: Acme Book Co., Supplement 1969), Section 341(b).

[4] Charles A. Lindquist, "An Analysis of Juror Selection Procedures in the United States District Courts" 4 *Temple Law Quarterly* 32 (1967), at 36.

[5] Jack Altman and Marvin Ziporyn, *Born to Raise Hell* (New York: Grove Press, 1968), p. 221.

[6] Adela Rogers St. Johns, *Final Verdict* (New York: Bantam Books, 1964), p. 344.

[7] Harold Norris, *A Casebook of Complete Criminal Trials* (Detroit: Citation Press, 1965), p. 1073.

[8] E.g., *Sellers v. United States,* 271 F.2d 475 (D.C.C.A. 1959).

[9] *Brown v. United States*, 338 F.2d 543 (D.C.C.A. 1964).

[10] *Sellers v. United States*, 271 F.2d 475 (D.C.C.A. 1959), at 446–447.

[11] Paul Holmes, *The Sheppard Murder Case* (New York: Bantam Books, 1962), pp. 59–60.

[12] St. Johns, *op. cit.*, p. 171.

[13] Floyd N. Heffron, *The Officer in the Courtroom* (Springfield, Ill.: Charles C Thomas, 1955), p. 13.

[14] See Lewis Mayers, *The American Legal System* (New York: Harper and Row, 1964), p. 39.

[15] *Ross v. United States*, 374 F.2d 97 (C.A. 8th Cir. 1967).

[16] Melvin M. Belli, *Ready for the Plaintiff* (New York: Popular Library, 1965), p. 279, tells of his disputes with the A.B.A. on this point.

[17] *Wall Street Journal*, January 13, 1969, pp. 1, 21.

[18] Harry Kalven, Jr., and Hans Zeisel, *The American Jury* (Boston: Little, Brown, 1966), p. 236.

[19] *Ibid.*, p. 239.

[20] See *The New York Times*, December 5, 1968, p. 94.

[21] It should in fairness be pointed out that the overwhelming majority of defendants are male too, except in certain specific crimes like shoplifting.

[22] Glanville Williams, *The Proof of Guilt*, 3rd ed. (London: Stevens, 1963), p. 272.

[23] Kalven, Jr., and Zeisel, *op. cit.*, p. 56.

[24] Jurors are reimbursed at the rate of $20 per day for federal jury service, but most state courts pay far less; in New York, it is $6 per day. *The New York Times*, December 5, 1968, pp. 49, 94.

[25] *Gregory v. United States*, 369 F.2d 185 (D.C.C.A. 1966).

[26] *Krulewitch v. United States*, 336 U.S. 440 (1949), at 453.

[27] *Wright v. State*, 325 P.2d 1089 (1958), at 1093.

[28] There is an excellent detailed discussion of inadmissible police testimony and its consequences in 8 A.L.R. 2d 1013.

[29] E.g., Rule 23, Federal Rules of Criminal Procedure. For a similar provision in a state constitution, see New York Constitution, Article I, section 2, and for a discussion of waiver in New York, see Lloyd I. Paperno and Arthur Goldstein, *Criminal Procedure in New York* (Massapequa, N.Y.: Acme Book Co., Supplement 1969), section 341 (a).

[30] See *Nick v. United States,* 122 F.2d 660 (1941).

[31] *Gaff v. State of Indiana,* 58 N.E. 74 (1900).

[32] *State v. Butts,* 159 S.W.2d 790 (1942). See also 140 A.L.R. 1177, where the whole subject of policemen and jury duty is discussed.

8 ★ On the Witness Stand

There are three parties in a criminal trial who are entitled to call witnesses—judge, prosecution, and defense. The right of a judge to call a witness is a legacy from earlier times, when in rural communities he might have personal knowledge of the parties. Today, a judge considers himself disqualified to try a case in which acquaintances of his are involved. The judge rarely exercises his right to call a witness. In practice, therefore, witnesses are called for the state or for the accused. Naturally, a police officer is normally called by the prosecution, because the evidence he can give tends to show that the accused is guilty. This chapter is written on the common-sense assumption that a police officer will be called as a witness for the state, but it should not be forgotten that occasionally the defense summons a police officer to testify on behalf of the accused. It may be believed that an officer has information favorable to the defense case.

No witness may choose which side he appears for; he is under a public duty to testify for whichever side subpoenas him. A *subpoena* is an order of the court, issued at the request of a party to litigation, which requires a citizen to appear and give evidence. It is perfectly possible for the defense to subpoena a police officer. Some district attorneys do not bother to subpoena police witnesses, but merely tell them to turn up at a particular time. This informality can sometimes be embarrassing, because an officer does not always get clear instructions, or forgets. Where no subpoena has been issued, the D.A. cannot complain if his witness does not appear. It is a better practice for all witnesses, whether policemen or not, to be subpoenaed.

WHY A WITNESS IS CALLED

Whichever side calls a witness does so because it hopes that questioning will elicit from the witness material helpful to its case.

The legal judgment upon this speculative question is influenced by many factors, most of which are dealt with in this book. Rules of evidence may prevent some valuable testimony from being given. Introduction of a witness who can aid one side's case may be undesirable because the same witness may also have information that is most detrimental to that side, or a witness may be of such bad character that he is not going to be believed.

Testimony is indispensable to a prosecutor; it is almost literally impossible for anyone who pleads not guilty in a criminal trial to be convicted without at least two witnesses for the prosecution appearing. Although there is no legal rule against convicting on the evidence of one witness, it is almost unknown in jury trials. The reason for this is that the burden of proof upon the prosecution is very heavy.

THE BURDEN OF PROOF

The prosecution must prove that the defendant is guilty *beyond reasonable doubt*. In the average case, this means that the prosecutor must pay attention to both the quality and the quantity of his evidence.

All legal systems have to lay down a standard of proof; it would not be acceptable if a person could be convicted of a crime because he *might* have done it. In Soviet Russia, the court must be *"convinced"* of the accused's guilt before conviction.[1] The difficulty with such phrases—whether American or Russian—is to know what they mean in practice. The general idea behind the words "beyond reasonable doubt" is clear enough. But what kind of doubt is reasonable?

A practical example will highlight the difficulty. Suppose that Smith is charged with housebreaking. He produces an alibi that at the material time he was with three friends playing cards. Let us further suppose that the three friends, who come to testify for his defense, are known to the police as undesirables. In the absence of really strong evidence that Smith did the housebreaking—e.g., fingerprints at the scene, or articles stolen from the house having been found in Smith's possession shortly afterward—is there a reasonable doubt? The jury does not need to believe the alibi in order to find a reasonable doubt. It may merely not be sure that the alibi is untrue.

The high burden of proof imposed on the prosecution adds to the work of the police. They have to prepare for all their evidence to be challenged; an accused is entitled to "the benefit of the doubt." Since "real evidence"—tangible things produced in court—is usually incontrovertible, defense counsel will seek to create doubt by undermining the prosecution's oral testimony. For this reason, police officers on the witness stand need to maintain a high standard.

THE RIGHT OF AN ACCUSED
TO REMAIN SILENT

The prosecution must produce all it can if it is going to obtain a conviction. What onus, if any, is there upon the defendant? The answer is: almost none.

At no stage may an accused be forced to cooperate in his own prosecution. He is entitled to sit quietly in court and say nothing. His testimony cannot be compelled; he has an absolute right to remain silent. Thus, the burden of proof upon the prosecution is even greater than at first appears. Not only must it prove its case beyond reasonable doubt, but it cannot rely upon the person who, the prosecution claims, knows most about the events in question! The prosecution cannot subpoena the defendant.

This rule has been inherited from the common law. It has long been criticized. As Jeremy Bentham put it: "If all the criminals of every class had assembled, and framed a system after their own wishes, is not this rule the very first which they would have established for their security? Innocence never takes advantage of it; innocence claims the right of speaking, and guilt invokes the privilege of silence." [2]

Neither the court nor prosecuting counsel may comment upon the accused's failure to testify. Bentham's view—that silence indicates guilt—cannot be expressed in the courtroom. Mr. Justice Douglas explained the reason for this rule in a 1965 Supreme Court decision, when he said that comment upon an accused's failure to testify would violate the Constitution because "it cuts down the privilege by making its assertion costly." [3] It is interesting to note that in England judges may comment upon such failure.

THE RIGHT OF AN ACCUSED TO TESTIFY

Nevertheless, the accused may choose to testify on his own behalf. If he goes into the witness-box, he can be questioned by his own lawyer, but after that the prosecution can question him. The rights of questioning a witness are more fully explained below.

The tactical position of the defense is complicated. If the accused is unlikely to make a good impression upon the witness stand, it will be best for him to exercise his right not to testify at all. On the other hand, if he does this, he may raise doubts in the minds of an intelligent jury: although neither the judge nor the prosecuting counsel is entitled to comment upon his nonappearance on the stand, the jury may nevertheless infer that he has chosen not to appear because he has something to hide. This is possible where a member of the jury has had previous experience on a jury, or is well educated and knows the legal position. Many lawyers believe that a jury will, in any case, hold it against a defendant if he does not take the stand. The famous nineteenth-century trial lawyer Earl Rogers always insisted that his clients did.[4] In modern times, 82 percent of defendants become witnesses at their own trials.[5]

If the accused does go on the stand, he must be prepared for questions from the prosecution. These will be designed to discredit him. Sometimes it does happen that an accused will completely vindicate himself by testimony that he chooses to give. In practice, however, that is unlikely, because if he can tell a story that shows his innocence, he is likely to have told it before the case ever came to trial. This is the practical working of Bentham's principle: most people will seek to avoid the embarrassment of a public trial. Nevertheless, a surprising number of criminal defendants "take pot luck" and testify at their own trials.

NO INQUISITION IN AMERICAN LAW

The importance of the accused's choice in going onto the witness stand lies in the absence of inquisitions in American law.

Most European systems of law permit the examination by a judge of those suspected of crime. The judge may ask a suspect nearly any question he chooses, whether it is designed to ascertain guilt or innocence or the social background of the suspect. All the answers that the defendant gives are recorded and may be used at his subsequent trial. In France, this judge is known as a *juge d'instruction*. An arrested person is brought before him by the police and he is under a duty to answer.

Thus, in the European systems, a substantial amount of material given by the accused himself is available by the time a trial takes place. By contrast, there is no judicial questioning procedure in the United States. Indeed, in general the judge here takes a much less dominant role in criminal proceedings than elsewhere. The only way in which an accused's words may be used to convict him in America is if he has "confessed" to the police and there are strict rules regarding the admissibility of such confessions into evidence.

It is worth noting, however, that the most straightforward means of ascertaining the truth is to ask the person who is accused of a crime. He, after all, probably knows more about it than anyone else. But the American trial system is not built to establish truth; rather it concentrates upon a narrower concept of proof.

Many police officers believe that interrogation is a necessary part of crime detection—and, indeed, perhaps it is. But except in limited circumstances police-induced confession is not acceptable in our courts. The police may not take for themselves the position of the inquisitorial judge in European proceedings. If they do, the courts will normally exclude evidence of any confession obtained thereby from the trial. Of course, where proceedings are not contemplated, interrogation can be extremely useful. Such a situation may arise where the suspect is insane and there is no chance that he will be tried.[6]

THE POSITION OF A WITNESS

Just as there is no inquisition of the accused in American trials, there is no inquisition of witnesses either. The court will rarely ask direct questions of a witness for the prosecution or defense. Questioning will be in the hands of counsel for either side. In general, the judge will ask a question only if there seems to be some confusion or misunderstanding as a result of counsels' questions.

One can explain the absence of inquisition of the accused in terms of fairness to him. But the absence of court questioning of a witness is more difficult to explain. Surely, if the courts have any concern with justice at all, they ought to probe the witnesses that both sides produce?

They do not because of the American belief that a trial should be an *adversary* proceeding. The theory is that if both sides are permitted to conduct their cases as they wish, there is no need for court intervention; the truth will appear from the conflict of prosecution and defense. This assumption is in reality a dubious one. There is no good reason for supposing that a presentation by two sides will disclose all there is to know. On the contrary, there may be matters that both prosecution and defense choose to suppress. In most cases, counsel are highly selective in what they elicit from witnesses. Sometimes, only a small part of what a witness knows of a case is revealed in court.

THE SEQUENCE OF QUESTIONING

The party that calls a witness questions him first. This process of questioning is known as *direct examination,* or *examination-in-chief.* In this examination, the side calling the witness will pose questions that reveal the purposes for which it has called the witness. This is important, because the other side can normally question the witness only upon matters arising out of direct examination and the implications flowing therefrom.

When the party calling the witness has finished his questions, the opposition may question the witness. The opposition is not bound to question, but a failure to do so may be taken as an admission that the witness's testimony is true. If the opposition side does choose to question him, the process is known as *cross-examination.*

In limited circumstances, the party calling the witness may re-question him after the opposition has cross-examined. The rules relating to this *re-examination* vary from state to state. Normally, questions on re-examination are confined to matters that have arisen as a result of cross-examination and that could not have been anticipated at the time of direct examination.

A police officer is most likely to be called by the prosecution, although as mentioned earlier, there is no reason why he should not be subpoenaed by the defense on occasion. However, it would amount to an abuse of the court if the defense were to subpoena a police officer in order to ensure that the prosecution could not use him. Strategically, it can sometimes be advantageous to call an officer and then ask him a few innocuous questions on the stand. Since the prosecution is confined on cross-examination to matters arising out of direct examination, it may not be able to ask the questions it wishes to. Some jurisdictions have specific rules forbidding the use of such practices by the defense. Others permit them, but allow the prosecution considerable latitude in cross-examination.

The sequence of direct examination, cross-examination, and re-examination can be gone through more than once with the same witness. It sometimes happens that a witness is called at an early stage. Later in the trial, it appears that matters within his knowledge, about which he has not testified, are going to be material in the case. In those circumstances, the court may give permission to re-call the witness.

The sequence may also be interrupted. If a witness is on the stand, he may be asked by the court to stop testifying in order that another witness may come to the stand immediately. This can sometimes happen when a witness has come to the court at great inconvenience and expense. It is better that he be brought to testify quickly, so that he can attend to his day-to-day affairs as soon as is practicable.

Where there is more than one defendant, the sequence may be modified. The prosecution will conduct its direct examination, and then each accused in turn has the right to cross-examine the witness.

PRIVILEGE IN COURT

This is the right of confrontation in action. For the period of the trial, the law regarding slander and libel is suspended. Counsel may ask questions that have clearly defamatory implications, and witnesses may reply with equal immunity from the law. The proceedings in court are *privileged*. Hence, a witness should not hesitate to speak out in court. He is legally protected, provided that he is not malicious in his accusations.[7]

This is a double-edged privilege. It means that a witness can say hard things about a defendant, but it also means that hard things may be said to and about a witness. It is sometimes said that no man involved in court proceedings comes out of them with a better reputation than he went in with. However tempting it may sometimes be, a police officer should always resist the temptation to say unpleasant things about an accused gratuitously. Not only does it lay him open to criticism from the bench, but it creates an unfortunate impression with the jury.

HOW A WITNESS MAY BE ATTACKED

One side in a lawsuit obviously wishes to undermine the witnesses the other side produces. This process is known as *impeachment*. A witness may be impeached by a showing that he is biased, that his character is bad, or that he has a bad reputation for veracity.

In practice, the only method of impeaching a police officer who has been called as a witness is by showing bias. A person of bad character, or one who is known as a liar, will not be a police officer. It is occasionally possible that a policeman's character is attacked, but such cases are rare.

Bias may be of two kinds: favor to the party calling the witness, or hostility toward the opposition. Such partiality may be alleged against police witnesses in criminal actions. The defense may allege that a police officer favors the prosecution, and that he greatly dislikes the accused. Indeed, in some jurisdictions, as explained in Chapter 7, page 91, it is within a trial judge's discretion to instruct the jury to guard against "the natural bias of police officers." [8]

However, warnings such as this are directed against policemen *as a class*. This section deals with ways in which an individual policemen may be impeached. Defense counsel may explore in cross-examination almost any evidence of bias. The fact that a policeman-witness was a good friend of the victim of the alleged crime, or a friend of the prosecuting attorney, might be exposed in order to show favor. Alternatively, hostility towards the accused could be shown if a witness owed him money, or had a grudge against him. These are only examples—all sorts of factors may indicate bias. As a leading authority has written: "The sources of partiality are too infinitely varied . . ." [9]

In order to avoid impeachment for bias, a policeman should avoid public statements before trial that could possibly be interpreted as partial. He should never allow himself to be drawn into discussions of a pending case by anyone, in case the defense subpoenas that person later to give an account of the conversation. Neither should he make any statement to the press that could conceivably be interpreted as biased. As explained in Chapter 15, page 205, such statements may be used in cross-examining by the defense.

An officer should also avoid even private expressions of opinion, or prejudiced statements, before trial. Remember that if a statement is made to only one person, in the most confidential circumstances, the defense may still subpoena that person to testify as to what was said. An example of the dangers of private acts tending to show bias before trial appears in a Colorado case, *Kidd v. People*, 51 P.2d 1020 (1935). Kidd was prosecuted and convicted for receiving stolen cigarettes and liquor, knowing them to have been stolen. Two important prosecution witnesses were a policeman and another man. The defense tried to impeach the policeman's testimony by proof that he had threatened to "pin something on" the other important prosecution witness if he refused to testify for the prosecution. Before making that threat, the policeman had kept the witness in jail for seventy-two hours, apparently entirely illegally. The judge refused to admit such evidence, but on appeal the conviction was reversed.

Several aspects of this case deserve note. First, the police officer concerned must obviously not have made his threat to the other witness publicly. Second, the evidence offered by the defense goes to show *both* kinds of bias: it shows undue keenness to aid the prosecution (to the extent of adopting illegal evidence) and bias against the accused, in that the policeman must have intended that the accused suffer, regardless of the merits of the prosecution.

Any officer who thinks he might be vulnerable to impeachment for bias should raise the matter with the public prosecutor *before* trial. The prosecutor can then decide how serious the possibility of impeachment is, and what tactics to adopt. There is no discredit attached to drawing attention to possible lines of attack the defense may use, and it is helpful to the prosecutor. It is the very kind of information he cannot acquire unless an officer consults him. In many important criminal cases, the defense spends substantial time and money looking for dirt to throw at prosecution witnesses. Minor things may be used to show bias. An officer should consider whether the defense has any ground for attacking him.

HOSTILE WITNESSES

Parties to a lawsuit choose witnesses because what they will say in court will aid their case. They predict what the witnesses will say from any pre-trial statement that a witness gave and from what the witness says during a pre-trial interview. But what happens when the witness does not say the things he has said before?

The law makes special provision for situations like this. If a party who calls a witness finds that his witness is unfavorably disposed to his client he may have him branded as a "hostile witness." If the court so brands him, he may be cross-examined by the party who has called him. As we have seen, in pages 110–111, the side that calls a witness is normally confined to *direct* examination, but where a witness is hostile the law makes an exception. An illustration from a criminal case will make the position clear.

In *State of Missouri v. Taylor*, 324 S.W.2d 643, 76 A.L.R. 2d 671 (1959), the defendant was accused of assault with intent to kill. The prosecution called a witness who had made statements that he had met the accused near the date of the alleged assault, and had noted that he had a gun stuck in his belt. This was important circumstantial evidence for the state. On the stand however, the witness showed a wholly uncooperative attitude toward the prosecution, and on direct examination he contradicted his previous statements. The prosecution, on application to the court, was permitted to cross-examine him about what had been said before.

It is extremely unlikely that a police officer would ever become a "hostile witness," whether he had been called for the prosecution or, as is sometimes possible, for the defense. Indeed, he would be acting unprofessionally if he did so. A hostile witness is not merely one who gives testimony unfavorable to the side that called him; he is one who has departed from the story that the side for which he appears reasonably believed he would tell. An officer of integrity will clearly not change his story on the witness stand.

Nevertheless, it is important that the police should understand the concept of a "hostile witness." They can aid the prosecution if they believe that one of its witnesses may not live up to expectations. Frequently, the police know when there is a danger that a witness may retract his statements in an effort to help the accused. Sometimes his motive is friendship; he wants to keep the accused out of prison. Sometimes a witness has been intimidated. Both matters may come to the attention of the police. They know of underworld loyalties, and they have a duty to investigate intimidation of prospective witnesses. When either of these possibilities exists, a police officer should warn the prosecutor. He can then decide what best suits the interest of the state: to call the witness, or to do without him, or to hope that the defense calls him instead.

NOTES

[1] Harold J. Berman, *Justice in the U.S.S.R.* (New York: Vintage Books, 1963), pp. 398–399.

[2] 3 Jeremy Bentham, *Rationale of Judicial Evidence* (London, 1827), pp. 131 *et seq.*

[3] *Griffin v. California*, 380 U.S. 609 (1965).

[4] Adela Rogers St. Johns, *Final Verdict* (New York: Bantam Books, 1964), p. 94.

[5] Harry Kalven, Jr., and Hans Zeisel, *The American Jury* (Boston: Little, Brown, 1966), p. 144.

[6] Such a situation arose with Albert DeSalvo, the self-confessed Boston Strangler. With the agreement of his defense counsel, he was questioned by police while he was a mental patient. The story he told left no doubt that he had committed the stranglings; his description of the victims and their apartments could have been given only by the killer. Interestingly, the interrogation in this case had to be carried out by the Assistant Attorney-General of Massachusetts, and not by the police officers investigating the case. If they had interrogated DeSalvo and he had confessed, the district attorneys of the counties that suffered the stranglings could have subpoenaed policemen to testify to the confession in court. See Gerold Frank, *The Boston Strangler* (New York: Signet Books, 1967), pp. 285–286.

[7] In many jurisdictions it has never been decided whether malicious statements in court are protected or not; but a cautious witness will not make his conduct the occasion of a decision.

[8] *Golliher v. United States*, 362 F.2d 594 (C.A. 8th Cir. 1966).

[9] Charles T. McCormick, *Handbook of the Law of Evidence* (St. Paul, Minn.: West Publishing Co., 1954), p. 83.

9 ★ Facing Opposition Council

In most cases, a police officer will appear for the prosecution. This chapter is written with that assumption. However, if he is called by the defense, the same principles apply. After testifying for whichever side calls him, he is open to cross-examination by opposing counsel.

Cross-examination is designed to diminish the value of what a witness has said on direct examination. Therefore, a "good" witness is one who stands up to cross-examination well. The side that calls a witness will take into account the possibility that he will respond poorly to cross-examination. But that is at best a guess; it is up to the witness personally to acquit himself well under cross-examination, because no one else can help him.

A word of warning is appropriate at this stage. An officer should never, under any circumstances, resort to lies under cross-examination. There are those who believe that "sometimes they [the police] convince themselves that a modicum of truth-stretching on their part could achieve the desirable end that strict adherence to the rules of evidence could not." [1] An officer who stoops to lying on the witness stand commits a criminal offense and demeans his profession.

PRE-TRIAL AID IN PREPARING FOR
CROSS-EXAMINATION

When a witness's testimony is going to be particularly valuable, counsel for the side that calls him will usually conduct a pre-trial interview. In this interview, he will indicate to his witness what questions he will ask in direct examination. He will also indicate what line he thinks the opposing lawyer will take in cross-examination. However, in dealing with the cross-examination, he will at most be making a shrewd guess. There is no obligation upon the parties litigant to disclose their trial tactics to each other. It may turn out that the lawyer who is calling a witness completely misjudges the thrust of the other side's argument. In that situation, a witness is truly alone when he faces cross-questioning.

When a police officer appears for the prosecution, he should be particular wary. First, district attorneys can spend less time preparing their witnesses than a private attorney; the pressure of work is just too much. Second, a district attorney will assume (rightly or wrongly) that a police officer is not so much in need of aid as a lay witness. Third, in criminal trials more than any other form of litigation, defense tactics are kept secret until revealed at trial. Except in a few jurisdictions, and in a few special instances, there is no obligation upon a criminal defendant to disclose his line of defense. An example of such an exception is the alibi. A New York statute imposes a duty upon a defendant to give notice to the prosecution if he will raise an alibi defense.[2] Even this, however, does not help the prosecution as much as might appear. It gives an opportunity to check on the defendant's whereabouts, but that is frequently such a difficult thing to do that no conclusive disproof can be found. As a New York D.A. explained it: "There is not a great deal that one can do to shake a well-presented alibi defense. Typically, some friends or relatives of the defendant affirm that the defendant attended a party or a card game on the night of the crime. The testimony is often quite convincing in its detail. The story has the ring of truth because in most cases the story is the truth, with only one fact changed—the date of the party or the card game." [3]

In the absence of a special statutory duty placed upon the defense, it can attack the prosecution as it likes. The guess a D.A. makes about the likely defense will be of value according to the nature of the case and his experience. No witness should forget, however, that it is a guess.

DIRECT EXAMINATION AS A BASIS OF CROSS-EXAMINATION

A police officer testifying for the prosecution probably knows in advance what the state prosecutor will ask. He should remember, however, that what really counts is his answers, not the questions. And it is not only what he says, but how he says it, that will affect the verdict.

While he is being cross-examined, the defense attorney will be watching for signs of weakness. There are four signs of weakness that a cross-examining lawyer is looking for: hesitation, evasion, stupidity, and inconsistency.

Lawyers are well aware of the significance of hesitation. A

legal text warns: ". . . the reluctance of witnesses to admit anything which may be inconsistent with their story as first given frequently manifests itself in hesitation in answering a question." [4] No officer should pretend to be certain of something if he is not. But he should ascend the witness stand knowing which parts of his testimony he is sure of and frankly admit which parts are unclear. The worst impression is created if he hesitates as if deciding which way to answer.

On no account should an officer appear to be ducking a question by his own counsel. The opposition will make a special note to follow up that question on cross-examination. Even if a truthful answer will weaken the prosecution case, or cast discredit upon the police force, or indeed upon the officer personally, it should be given candidly.

Whether reasonably or not, a fault readily confessed is much more palatable than one concealed. This is particularly true with a court witness, because if he appears evasive upon one unsavory aspect of his testimony, a jury may infer that nothing he says is reliable.

An officer faced with giving testimony that he would prefer not to give should realize that what he wishes to avoid may not appear bad to a jury. Witnesses tend to be oversensitive on the stand, whoever they are. Anyone who has seen testimony given in a divorce case, where the parties have to deal with intimate and unpleasant matters, will know that the witness apparently suffers much more embarrassment than his audience. In the same way, an officer may feel that something is discreditable much more than a layman will. No witness can be objective about his testimony. There is something about being on the witness stand that many people find discomforting. A famous trial lawyer, Melvin Belli, has described the sensitivity of some witnesses:

People are quite likely to undergo a rather weird "sea change" when they step into the witness chair. A young woman who appears confident and assured in my office, and who answers questions clearly and intelligently under those circumstances, may become almost unrecognizable on the stand. She is embarrassed about being up there "in front of all those people." . . . A particularly aggressive cross-examination may cause her to break down altogether. Yet her cause may be absolutely just, her claims completely honest.[5]

Even an experienced policeman may suffer the same sort of "stage fright" as is described here.

This embarrassment that many witnesses feel can be ascribed to the public nature of American criminal trials. A witness exposes himself not only to the judge and jury, but often to a good number of spectators and pressmen. The guarantee of public trial in the Constitution was inserted in order to prevent Star Chamber practices from developing in the United States. However, it is sometimes questioned whether the use of public trial is necessary to achieve this end. Some commentators fear that the presence of public and press at trials encourages witnesses to be more concerned with making a good impression on their audience than with accurately recalling what they have been called to tell the court.[6] The sensible course for a police witness is to concentrate upon winning the jury and to let the members of the public who are present form whatever impression they wish. In practice, it will probably be as favorable or unfavorable as the jury's.

A policeman faced with testifying to matters that he feels, for whatever reason, reluctant to express, will do much better to state them directly than to appear evasive. It is not only dishonorable to shape an answer in order to conceal a fact, but it is bad tactics. It allows opposition counsel to make capital from gaining a reluctant admission on cross-examination. If an officer answers directly, on the other hand, the jury will be impressed with his fairness, and any adverse fact brought out will have minimum impact.

Stupidity is something the most intelligent person can be guilty of occasionally, especially on the witness stand. Nervousness may trap the most sensible witness into saying silly things.

A famous example, known to lawyers on both sides of the Atlantic, occurred in the Laski libel action in England, directly after the Second World War. Harold Laski, a socialist politician, had made a speech during an election campaign. A newspaper had reported that Mr. Laski had "advocated revolution." Laski sued the newspaper for libel, and in trying to show that he had not advocated revolution, called as his witness Vice-Admiral Sir Hugh de Crespigny, who had been present at the meeting. On direct examination, Sir Hugh testified that Mr. Laski had not advocated revolution. He was then cross-examined:

Q: Are you a little deaf?
A: Yes, a little.
Q: Then how do you know what Mr. Laski said?
A: Oh, I was near to him and I don't miss much.
Q: But you missed some?
A: I would have missed nothing important.
Q: If you missed some, how can you tell whether it was important or not?
A: Please let me explain . . .
Q: No further questions.

Since counsel for the opposition has the right to cease questioning when he pleases, Sir Hugh had at that time to stand down. The result was that he looked a fool, although he was an honest and intelligent man.

This was a lucky strike for counsel, who was extremely quick to seize his advantage. Nevertheless, it serves as an illustration of the dangers of an unfortunate answer from a witness. The effect of this trouncing cross-examination was to render all that Sir Hugh had said on direct examination doubtful. A witness should avoid unthinking answers such as this witness gave.

Inconsistency on the witness stand—the fourth of the weaknesses a cross-examining lawyer is looking for—is so important that it requires a section to itself.

INCONSISTENCY

Of all the powerful arguments that a lawyer hopes to put to a jury, perhaps the commonest is "this witness is inconsistent." A defense lawyer who has a basis for such an argument will say that the witness's testimony cannot be relied upon because he has not stuck to one story. Therefore, there is a reasonable doubt and the accused must be acquitted.

It is not necessary that the defense accuse a witness of being dishonest. It is enough to point to inconsistencies and leave it to the jury to decide whether they are caused by dishonesty or faulty memory.

Does it happen frequently that a witness tells inconsistent stories? The answer is that it does. Of course, it is not common that a witness says one thing and then a completely different thing five minutes later—though it does occur; but a cross-examining lawyer is frequently armed with records of what a witness said about the case on occasions prior to the trial. Very often, there are discrepancies between the reports of previous statements and testimony on the witness stand. A lawyer will use these in an attempt to show a witness unreliable. Louis Nizer, a well-known trial lawyer, used to collect all statements made by a witness prior to trial. Then, he would put the statements in parallel columns and underline every little difference. He used this as a guide to cross-examining the witness on the stand.

This form of cross-examination is particularly effective when there has been some delay between the commission of the crime and the trial. Every time a lawyer finds a contradiction, he can use it to reinforce his argument that a witness cannot be relied upon because he has forgotten the events to which he is trying to testify. In making such an argument, lawyers are playing upon the ignorance of the psychology of memory that most jurymen suffer. There is much modern research to indicate that memory is *not* accurate and that the mind deals with hazy areas of memory by inventing plausible "bridges" between one clearly imprinted image and another. Almost certainly, variations will appear in a person's recall if he is asked about an event at intervals. It may be true that, ultimately, the courts place too much reliance on memory; but in the absence of alternative means of proof, the system is not likely to change. In addition, although the argument about the fallibility of memory is often used, juries frequently convict nevertheless. Perhaps, therefore, defense lawyers are optimistic, and juries know more about memory than they think!

THE SOURCE OF PRIOR STATEMENTS

To show inconsistency with prior statements, a cross-examining lawyer must have records from which to compare what a witness says in court with what he said before. It might seem strange that he should have them; in fact, however, he is often able to procure them.

In some states, there is a duty upon the prosecution to turn over reports upon which they rely to the defense. Obviously, these will include statements made by witnesses at various times. In addition, defense lawyers may in some states be entitled to copies of grand jury testimony.[7] The grand jury is the jury to which the prosecution presents its case in order to persuade it to issue an indictment. Hence, a good part of the prosecution evidence will have a preview before the grand jury. Since grand jury proceedings frequently occur months before trial, there is opportunity for minor variations to appear in what even an honest prosecution witness says. Less honest witnesses will sometimes repudiate their grand jury testimony entirely when confronted with it later.[8]

Some jurisdictions allow limited access to police reports directly.

Apart from such official sources, a defense attorney may glean reports from local newspapers to which witnesses, including police officers, spoke, or from private individuals to whom witnesses told the story.

AVOIDING INCONSISTENCY

A policeman should prepare for trial exactly as an opposition attorney does. If there are many prior statements, he should draw up columns in which statements about the facts appear opposite one another. He too should underline the inconsistencies. This is a situation where it pays to "know thine enemy."

What should a witness do if he finds inconsistencies in his previous statements? He cannot hide them (which would be dishonest anyway); rather, he should think about the reasons for the inconsistency. If he cannot find a reason, he must admit it on the stand. True, if the inconsistency is large, this will still enable a defense lawyer to score his point about the fallibility of memory. But much of the effect will be lost. The witness will not be taken aback when confronted with the inconsistency, and hence his temptation to bluster his way out of the contradiction will be minimized.

An officer should readily admit that his memory has dimmed with the passing of time. It is natural that it should. Too many witnesses, sensing a trap, pretend that it has not. In doing this, a policeman would appear "prosecution oriented" and lay himself open to doubt. In some situations, it is greatly to a witness's advantage to admit that his memory is shaky. He is entitled to "refresh his recollection" while on the witness stand from a report which he made at the time of the events that he witnessed. This takes a considerable strain off a witness who is dealing with events some time in the past. A police officer's notebook or first report back at the station house is normally acceptable in these circumstances.

USE OF CONTEMPORANEOUS MEMORANDA
BY WITNESS

A witness may not read a prepared statement from the witness stand. However, in most jurisdictions, he may refresh his memory by referring to a report made at the time. With the permission of the court, he may have it at his side while testifying and refer to it, provided he does not rely on it. In such an instance, the report itself is not put in evidence.[9]

If the witness cannot remember what happened at all, and his memory is not jogged by looking at his report, the report itself may be put in evidence.

These rules underline the importance of making good reports at the time events take place. They can aid an officer on the witness stand and sometimes become part of the evidence. In this way, the harm done by loss of memory is minimized.

It should be noted that where a contemporaneous report is admitted into evidence, the opposition is practically denied the right to cross-examine. The report itself cannot be questioned, and the witness who made it has no memory of the events at all. Thus, a well-prepared report may have a more devastating effect upon the opposition than a witness's recollection. This is discounted in part by the fact that a written report will rarely be accepted so readily by a jury as personal testimony on the stand. But it is one of the peculiarities of the rules of evidence that where a contemporaneous report has been made, it is sometimes tactically advantageous that a witness remember nothing! By confessing a complete memory blank, he permits his report to get into evidence, whereas if he remembers shakily, his report cannot be evidence, and his memory may be discredited under cross-examination.

WHY LAWYERS LOOK FOR INCONSISTENCY

Lawyers love inconsistencies because they often provide the only line of attack that the defense can make. In most prosecutions, there is little evidence a defendant can produce to show innocence. Therefore, his counsel must concentrate upon shaking the state's case. Inconsistencies are relatively easy to find, and they form a basis for arguing that "reasonable doubt" exists.

As mentioned earlier, the only justification for prosecution that an overworked police department and district attorney's office has is the hope of a conviction. Therefore any case that comes to trial is one that the D.A. thinks strong. That means that the defense case is weak. Defense attorneys know that most of their courtroom work is fighting a losing battle, but it is their duty to fight the battle as well as possible for their client. They seek to discredit prosecution witnesses as part of that duty. That is why many policemen get the feeling that they, not the defendants, are being tried. But much of the effect of showing inconsistency can be minimized if police witnesses have studied their own prior statements and know where contradictions occur. By doing so, they ensure that they are prepared for cross-examination and can make the best possible impression in court.

In Chapter 4, pages 44–46, officers were recommended to keep copies of all their reports. On page 127 we noted that lawyers sometimes acquire material for cross-examination from local newspaper stories. Sometimes, a police officer makes a statement to the press about the case. Whenever he does so, he should ask the reporter to send him a copy of the report as it appears in the newspaper. Unless he does, he is not entitled to a copy; when someone makes a voluntary statement, it becomes the property of the person taking the statement, in the absence of any arrangement to the contrary.[10] An officer who asks for such cooperation from the press will serve two purposes: (1) he will avoid being surprised on the witness stand if a defense lawyer puts a newspaper report of what he said to him, and (2) he will be informed about the nature of the publicity that a case has received. The importance of this is explained in Chapter 15, *Publicity and Testimony*.

SEQUESTRATION

Since the main purpose of cross-examination is to expose inconsistency and therefore cast reasonable doubt on the evidence, a defense attorney has an interest in maximizing the chance that inconsistency will appear. Naturally a witness who sits in court and listens to what other witnesses on his side say is at an advantage when he reaches the stand. He knows what the evidence so far presented indicates, and he can modify his testimony to fall in line with it. Whether he does so consciously (which would be dishonest) or unconsciously, he is taking away opposition counsel's ammunition.

In order to prevent this, a defense attorney may ask that a particular prosecution witness, or prosecution witnesses in general, shall be excluded from the courtroom until they are called to give evidence. This exclusion is called *sequestration*.

Sequestration helps to preserve inconsistencies between witnesses, because one witness cannot know what another has said if he was not present in court while the other testified. Many legal authors have regarded sequestration as an essential safeguard against perjury. One expert wrote that "the expedient of sequestration is (next to cross-examination) one of the greatest engines that the skill of man has ever invented for the detection of liars in a court of justice." [11]

No sequestration will take place unless prosecution or defense requests it. Neither of them may demand it as a right; it is within the discretion of the trial judge. A request for exclusion may be confined to one witness, or may include all witnesses. When a witness has been ordered to remain outside court until he testifies, he is said to be "under the rule." A refusal to grant "the rule" may be a ground for ordering retrial if the defendant was prejudiced thereby.

There is a large amount of case law upon sequestration, and it is worth mentioning that it could all be avoided if American courts would adopt the English practice. In England, it is not necessary to ask for sequestration, since it is understood automatically that all prospective witnesses should keep out of court until they are called. As the English court of appeal, criminal division, stated recently: ". . . the general rule and practice in criminal cases is that witnesses as to fact on each side should remain out of court until they are required to give evidence. The reason for this is obvious. It is that if they are permitted to hear the evidence of other witnesses they may be tempted to trim their own evidence." [12]

In most jurisdictions in the United States, there is no such general rule. As a result, special rules have grown up regarding sequestration and its effect upon police officers. Even where the trial court has granted a general exclusion of prosecution witnesses from the courtroom, police officials may not be bound by it. Where a peace officer is under a legal duty to attend all court sessions (as sheriffs in Arizona are), he is entitled to remain in court even though he was not expressly excluded from sequestration and even though he is going to give evidence for the state.[13] An officer who is necessary for the organization of the prosecution case may also ignore a sequestration order, even though he is to be called as a witness.[14] One case appears to hold that an officer shall be immune from general sequestration orders simply because he has sat at counsels' table throughout the trial.[15]

The general attitude of the courts, however, is that police can ignore exclusion rules only if they have a special reason for being in the courtroom. They have no special immunity from sequestration. Thus, where a total exemption for police witnesses was claimed, an Oklahoma court rejected the possibility, saying that "no good reason appears to us as to why they [the police] should have been exempted from a general rule applicable to all of the witnesses." [16]

Of course, where the court makes a specific exclusion rule, applying to particular police officers, they should comply with it. Sometimes they should remain outside the courtroom even when a trial judge has refused to sequester them in order to avoid giving the defense a ground for appeal. The trial judge might be found wrong in his refusal by an appellate court, but it will be "harmless error" if the defense cannot show some prejudice, and there will be no prejudice if the officers concerned voluntarily kept out of court. An illustration of the dangers comes from the leading Pennsylvania case of *Commonwealth v. Turner*.[17] In a trial for murder, the defense asked that one police officer be excluded from court while the other gave evidence for the prosecution. The prosecution's major effort was directed toward proving that the accused had made an inculpatory statement to his cellmate after arrest. The two officers concerned with the sequestration motion claimed to have overheard the remark. The defense wanted one officer outside the courtroom while the other gave evidence because it feared that if they were both present in court they would make their testimony agree exactly. Sequestration was refused and the accused was convicted. On appeal, the conviction was overturned. The appellate court stated that this was a situation in which the *credibility* of the two officers was most important and that the refusal of sequestration had prejudiced the accused's chances of attacking credibility.

In view of the room for dispute that exists in the law of sequestration, police officers should adopt the following courses. If a general order for sequestration is made, which does not expressly exempt police officers, the police officers should leave the courtroom; there is no harm in being particularly careful. If an officer has a special reason for remaining in court, he should communicate with prosecuting counsel immediately. The prosecutor can then request that the court explicitly grant permission that the officer remain. If a specific request for sequestration is made and granted, the officer concerned will of course absent himself from court until he is called as a witness. But even if a specific request is refused, the officer should consider leaving voluntarily; trial judges can be wrong, as the *Turner* case shows. Since police officers are professionally interested in avoiding giving a defendant grounds for appeal, they might with advantage take this specially cautious step.

After an officer has testified, it is perfectly proper for him to remain in court and hear the rest of the case, if he wishes. Occasionally, complications arise when a prosecution witness is recalled to rebut a suggestion made by the defense, but this is rare. Since the law permits a witness to be called on rebuttal only when the prosecution could not reasonably have foreseen the defense, a witness who has been called cannot reasonably foresee that he will be recalled.

POLICE OFFICERS IN THE COURTROOM
WHO ARE NOT WITNESSES

In all jurisdictions, it is usual to have a law-enforcement officer present in the courtroom. Generally this creates no difficulty, but problems can arise. A peace officer who is a witness and remains in the courtroom may be subject to sequestration, as explained above; this section deals with police officers who are not witnesses, but who nevertheless attend court proceedings.

A police officer should beware of hindering the defense in any way. If he does so, intentionally or inadvertently, the result may be a mistrial. An example of a claim of inadvertent obstruction of the defense is contained in *Cooper v. Denno*, 129 F. Supp. 123, 221 F.2d 626 (1955), a New York case that was finally appealed to the federal courts. The defendants were on trial for murder, of which they were convicted. The police feared that during the trial the defendants might try to escape, and so the courtroom was heavily guarded. The defendants and their attorney chose to speak Yiddish while consulting in court. After conviction, they raised objection to the close proximity to counsel's table of a police officer who understood Yiddish and claimed that he had overheard the confidential conversations of lawyer and client and reported them to the prosecutor.

The defendants' claim was rejected by the federal court of appeals on three grounds: first, the police officer concerned denied having heard any conversation or reporting it to the prosecutor; second, the defendants had made no attempt during trial to lower their voices and therefore to avoid being overheard; third, they had raised no objection to the officer's closeness to the counsel table during trial. Nevertheless, this ground of appeal took the defendants through the New York state appellate courts and two federal courts; the waste of time and public money was huge. To avoid this, police officers should be careful that nothing they do in the courtroom will give the defense a ground to appeal.

No comprehensive list of things to avoid can be given, because the ingenuity of defense counsel can never be wholly anticipated, but among them must be attempts to overhear or oversee defense material; registering reactions of approval of prosecution witnesses, or disapproval of defense witnesses, within sight of the jury; speaking to jurors, or distracting defense counsel from presenting his case. All these forms of conduct would have to be extreme before they could raise a ground of appeal, but they are nevertheless to be discouraged. And, as *Cooper v. Denno* shows, a policeman must not only not do these things, but avoid appearing to do them.

DEFENSE TACTICS IN CROSS-EXAMINATION

By and large, lawyers have no formal training in trial technique. They learn it by experience, if at all. Nevertheless, there are works that instruct criminal lawyers in trial work, and a police officer should be aware of them. They usually offer advice on how to deal with particular kinds of witnesses, including police officers. A policeman who knows what lawyers' books recommend to lawyers is better prepared to handle himself well on the witness stand than most. Here is one significant passage from a trial textbook:

> [Police officer] witnesses will normally try to determine the motive behind your questions [on cross-examination] before they answer. Keep your questions disconnected. Use the jump-around technique. Put your questions rapidly so he cannot keep up with you. If you can keep him in the dark as to the motives and reasons for your questions, he may succumb more easily.
>
> Police officers are generally careless as to the form and manner in which they noted statements made to them. Generally they add a great deal to their testimony besides what they have noted. Dwell at length upon their failure to write down the statements the defendant is alleged to have made. Carefully examine any notations they did make. Question them about any testimony that is not found in their notes.
>
> Generally, follow this negative approach throughout your cross-examination. In other words, point up what they *failed* to do or see, not what they claimed they did or saw.[18]

This advice is typical of the way in which some defense lawyers think. A police officer may draw his own conclusions from the passage quoted as to the worth of the advice. But whatever its worth, an officer should bear in mind that if an adversary's strategy is anticipated, it is defeated. Defense lawyers are advised to ask questions quick-fire, so that a police witness "cannot keep up." Therefore, an officer should refuse to be pushed through cross-examination; he should give his answers slowly, so that he gains time to think. The advice regarding police "carelessness" in keeping notes of what has been said may seem unfair. Yet since defense lawyers wish to dwell upon such matters, an officer should be careful to put all relevant material in his reports. Here is an example of the way that pre-trial preparation paves the way to effective courtroom testimony.

THE POWER OF CROSS-EXAMINATION

Cross-examination is by no means the powerful weapon it is sometimes portrayed to be for the detection of error or falsehood in witnesses. In spite of much that has been written in its praise, cross-examination rarely penetrates an out-and-out lie and cannot expose the really dishonest.

Practically, lawyers use it to undermine testimony that is admittedly honestly given; they do not expect to uncover perjury, though on occasion they do. The power of cross-examination is severely reduced when a witness has experience and knows the system; most victories are won from witnesses who are ill at ease and flustered because they do not know what to expect. An experienced witness is generally invulnerable. This is recognized in many of the manuals for lawyers; one that includes policemen in its category of "professional witnesses" says: "A professional witness's testimony is difficult to break down on cross-examination. Often he anticipates the very question and practically always has a ready answer." [19]

The explanation might be, of course, that an experienced witness tells the truth anyway. But is that not usually true of inexperienced witnesses too? The real distinguishing feature of these witnesses is that they are self-assured and do not begin with a crippling fear of what may happen to them under questioning. They are not intimidated by their surroundings or the prospect of being interrogated. As one lawyer pointed out, to picture the average attorney as a masterful, competent advocate is utterly absurd; he is usually inexperienced and just as nervous as the person he has to question.[20] The fear that strikes many witnesses comes from an overestimation of the impact of cross-examination and an underestimation of their ability to sustain it. Jerry Giesler, the famous Hollywood defense attorney, with a great reputation as a shrewd cross-examiner, used to get so nervous as to become physically sick before his trials.[21]

GAMES DEFENSE ATTORNEYS PLAY

There are two practices that some defense lawyers resort to in cross-examining police witnesses that can be annoying. The first is refusing to address an officer-witness by his rank (e.g., "officer" or "sergeant"), and the second is deliberately mispronouncing the officer's name. It would be pleasant to report that these childish games are rare, but unfortunately they are not. A leading text for trial lawyers advises:

> Police witnesses should always be addressed as "Mr." rather than "officer" or "detective." Such a practice helps dispel many jurors' mistaken notion that there is something sacrosanct about a policeman on the stand, and aids in reducing him to his proper stature as a witness.[22]

A book for police officers states that the deliberate mispronunciation of a witness's name is "common." [23]

Both tactics are designed to annoy the witness and if possible make him show some temper on the stand. However, a police officer should resist all temptation to object or to correct the defense lawyer. Above all, he should in no circumstances retaliate by mispronouncing the lawyer's name. The dignified and proper course is to ignore the antics of such lawyers, thereby implying that their tactics are beneath consideration.

It may be some consolation to an officer who is treated in this rude fashion that lawyers have been known to treat each other in the same immature manner. During the trial of Jack Ruby, the prosecutor for a time referred to defense counsel by a mispronounced name. Since defense counsel was one of the most famous lawyers in the country, there was no possibility that this was an innocent error.[24]

ANTAGONISM DURING CROSS-EXAMINATION

Cross-examination brings out a combative instinct in both lawyers and witnesses. The cross-examiner wants to trap the witness and the witness knows it. The witness resents the implication behind some of the questions that he is untruthful, or mistaken. Even where a witness has no material interest in the outcome of litigation, cross-examination has the effect of making him take sides.

From the lawyer's viewpoint, cross-examination is a way of using witnesses who are not his in order to benefit his client. Cross-examination allows a lawyer to prey upon a flustered witness, to cajole and browbeat him if it serves his client's interest. A lawyer is prohibited from gratuitous rudeness, but he has no obligation to be polite, and many defense lawyers are not. The result is sometimes that tempers rise in lawyer and witness alike.

Police witnesses should be especially careful not to be goaded into anger on the stand, for anger can warp judgment. The golden rule is never to lose one's temper on the witness stand, to meet rudeness with exemplary good manners, to remain unprovoked by provocation. No witness— and least of all a policeman—will improve his chances of persuading the jury by losing control. A jury will respect a witness who resists attacks with dignity far more than one who lashes out in retaliation. Words spoken in anger on the witness stand can never be retracted. A coroner with wide experience as a prosecution witness used to carry a note to himself in his pocket whenever he testified, which read "Don't lose your temper." Police witnesses should follow this example.[25]

NOTES

[1] Melvin M. Belli, *Dallas Justice* (New York: David McKay Co., 1964), p. 157.

[2] See Kevin Tierney, "Notice of Alibi" 118 *New Law Journal* 463 (1968).

[3] David Worgan and Monrad Paulsen, "The Position of a Prosecutor in a Criminal Case" 7 *Practical Lawyer* 43 (1961), at 57.

[4] William Henry Gallagher, *Technique of Cross-Examination* (New York: Practicing Law Institute, 1962), p. 73.

[5] Melvin M. Belli, *Ready for the Plaintiff* (New York: Popular Library, 1965), p. 89.

[6] E.g., Lewis Mayers, *The American Legal System* (New York: Harper & Row, 1964), pp. 110–111.

[7] Not all states require indictments to be authorized by a grand jury; some permit magistrates or lower-court judges to issue indictments. In such cases, the prosecution still has to show the evidence upon which it seeks an indictment, and the defense may be entitled to copies of the testimony given in the lower-court proceedings.

[8] See, for example, *The New York Times*, November 9, 1968, p. 9, for a New Jersey case in which a woman witness in a murder trial denied the story she gave to the grand jury, excusing herself on the ground that she feared for her own life if she were to tell the truth.

[9] *Miller v. Borough of Exeter*, 77 A.2d 395; 366 Pa. 336 (1951). This Pennsylvania case involved a civil action over an accident on a sidewalk.

[10] Belli, *op. cit.*, footnote 5, p. 233.

[11] *Wigmore on Evidence*, 3rd ed., section 1838, p. 354.

[12] *R. v. Joan Smith* [1968] 2 A11 E.R. 115. [1968] 1 W.L.R. 636, discussed in 128 *Journal of Criminal Law* 242 (1968).

[13] *People v. Chapman*, 209 P.2d 121 (1949) (Cal.).

[14] *State v. Thomas*, 275 P.2d 408 (1954) (Ariz.).

[15] *Roberson v. United States*, 282 F.2d 648 (1960).

[16] *Thompson v. State*, 118 P.2d 269 (1941) (Okla.).

[17] *Commonwealth v. Turner*, 88 A.2d 915 (1952) (Pa.). The case is discussed in 32 A.L.R. 2d 358.

[18] Henry B. Rothblatt, *Successful Techniques in the Trial of Criminal Cases* (New York: Prentice-Hall, 1961), p. 71. This book is written exclusively from the point of view of defense lawyers; it begins, "Your client has been arrested" (p. 3).

[19] Jules H. Baer and Simon Balicer, *Cross-Examination and Summation*, 2nd ed. (New York: Fallon Law Book Co., 1948), p. 88.

[20] Charles L. Cusumano, *Laugh at the Lawyer Who Cross-Examines You* (New York: Old Faithful Publishing Co., 1942), p. 3.

[21] Jerry Giesler, *Hollywood Lawyer* (New York: Pocket Books, 1962), pp. 87, 95.

[22] 13 *Am. Jur. Trials* 527.

[23] Floyd N. Heffron, *The Officer in the Courtroom* (Springfield, Ill.: Charles C Thomas, 1955), p. 97.

[24] John Kaplan and Jon Waltz, *The Trial of Jack Ruby* (New York: The Macmillan Co., 1965), p. 103.

[25] Paul Holmes, *The Sheppard Murder Case* (New York: Bantam Books, 1962), p. 91.

10 ★ The Defense of Entrapment

In many jurisdictions, including the federal one, a criminal defendant may avoid conviction by showing that police conduct amounted to an "entrapment."

THE MEANING OF ENTRAPMENT

There are differing definitions of entrapment in use at the present time. The essence of the defense is that police conduct induced the defendant to commit the acts that amount to the crime charged. A typical state-court definition comes from a Virginia report: "The act of officers or agents of the government in inducing a person to commit a crime not contemplated by him, for the purpose of instituting a criminal prosecution against him." [1]

The defense is only available when it is alleged that policemen or other government agents induced the crime: "The doctrine . . . does not extend to acts of inducement on the part of a private citizen who is not an officer of the law." [2]

Entrapment defenses are common in prosecutions involving such things as narcotics trafficking. Wherever undercover agents are used, there is a danger that the police will be accused of entrapment. The difficulty with entrapment is that sometimes the borderline between entrapment and merely giving the opportunity to commit a crime is vague.

SHERMAN v. UNITED STATES

A leading Supreme Court case, *Sherman v. United States*,[3] illustrates what amounts to entrapment. A Treasury agent met an addict in a doctor's surgery. The addict was there to be treated for his addiction. The narcotics agent pretended to be an addict himself and acted as if he were suffering greatly from drug deprivation. The real addict was sympathetic, but refused to sell the agent any drugs. After three such meetings in the surgery, the addict relented, after the agent had described his great suffering, and supplied drugs. A consequence of the agent's pleading was that the real addict, who was on the way to a cure, also started taking drugs again.

The Supreme Court reversed the addict's conviction for drug trafficking. The agent's conduct amounted to entrapment under federal law. He had not merely provided an opportunity for the crime to be committed, but had actually encouraged it.

The court based its decision upon the fact that police conduct was "unconscionable."

THE UNIQUE NATURE OF
THE ENTRAPMENT DEFENSE

There is no other defense known to the criminal law that allows acquittal on the ground of police conduct.

A police officer involved in a case in which entrapment is raised has a special responsibility to acquit himself well, because it challenges directly the policy of the police department as a whole.

The defense represents an exception to normal rules of legal culpability. Lawyers normally divide up the elements of a crime into *actus reus* and *mens rea*. *Actus reus* means, literally, the "guilty act." The guilty act is all those things done that are necessary elements of the offense charged. *Mens rea* is the intention to commit those acts. Normally, a person is assumed to intend his acts and their likely consequences, and therefore, provided the acts are proved, the intention may be assumed. There are some exceptions to this rule—e.g., where insanity is pleaded, or where the defendant claims he was sleepwalking, or drunk—but they are in practice rarely encountered.

In entrapment situations, however, the presumption of intention is not rebutted, but merely ignored. The defendant admits all the acts necessary to prove the crime and does not claim that he did not intend those acts; he merely says that police encouragement provided him with an excuse. This plea is greatly criticized by some lawyers and law-enforcement officials, but nevertheless is recognized in the courts as a valid defense. Accordingly, a defendant may say "I admit I did it, and by normal principles of law I am guilty, but the police have behaved so badly that their conduct has cancelled out my own crime."

THE NECESSITY FOR CAREFUL
POLICE PLANNING

Officers who contemplate participating in undercover work should carefully consider whether their plan will amount to entrapment. If necessary, a police department should take legal advice before acting. Usually, the state prosecutor will be able to give an opinion on the matter. If he approves a course of action, the police department will be protected.

There are several factors which should be considered before embarking upon a plan that might raise entrapment questions. First, the department should consider whether evidence of the crime they are investigating could be acquired without resort to methods that may raise entrapment. Second, they should avoid using means of persuasion that put great pressure upon the suspect. The mistake made by the police in the *Sherman* case was to appeal to the suspect's good nature. If Sherman had merely been asked in the doctor's waiting room for a supply of drugs and had given it without reluctance, there is no doubt his conviction would have been upheld. The agent would at most have provided simple opportunity. Third, the police should attempt detection that may come close to entrapment only if they have reason to believe that the person they may finally apprehend is truly an important criminal. In no other legal defense is it possible to bring so much disrepute to a police force as entrapment. No policeman should lightly embark upon a course of action that, if considered in court, may discredit his department's judgment.

DEALING WITH ENTRAPMENT IN COURT

Where entrapment is raised by the accused, he will be emphasizing police conduct more than is common. All the principles of police testimony will apply in added measure in this situation. Answers should be direct and candid, and no officer should shirk from explaining exactly how the detection took place. If he appears to be hiding something, the court may believe there is something to hide.

Although many officers form the impression that courts are more against the police than against criminals, the entrapment defense proves otherwise. In general, unless the police have inveigled a defendant into committing a crime, the courts will uphold police conduct and convict the accused. The entrapment defense involves, of necessity, the admission by the accused that he did the prohibited acts and unless it appears that the police implanted the criminal purpose in a defendant's mind, the court will convict.

There is a legal difficulty that has not been surmounted with regard to entrapment. One of the factors that may lead the police to resort to undercover methods in order to gain evidence will be the previous record of the accused. If he is known to indulge in a particular form of criminal activity, because he has prior convictions the police may feel justified in resorting to exceptional detection methods. Yet, normally, a defendant's previous convictions cannot be disclosed at trial. Therefore the police cannot refer to them. However, this problem has largely been dealt with by the appeal courts. If a defendant is convicted, in spite of raising the entrapment defense, the appeal court may consider previous convictions in deciding whether to affirm or quash a conviction. At appeal level, witnesses do not appear, because the appeal will be taken on the transcript of trial evidence. Even if the police cannot advert to previous convictions at trial, they will do so before the appellate court.

JURY ATTITUDES TOWARD ENTRAPMENT

On page 144 we noted the legal definition of entrapment. The police should realize, however, that legal definitions are governing only if the jury accepts them. If it does not, it may return a verdict which is not in accordance with the letter of the law. There is evidence to suggest that juries sometimes go beyond the strict meaning of entrapment and acquit where the police have done something of which the jurors disapprove. One study has concluded that the jury is "expanding the legal doctrine of entrapment." [4] Thus, a jury acquitted an accused of drunken driving when the police stood by and watched the defendant stagger into his automobile and drive away. The judge in this instance thought that the jury acquitted because "the sheriff could have prevented the defendant from committing the crime." [5] Yet, of course, the conduct of the sheriff did not amount to entrapment in the legal sense.

NOTES

[1] *Falden v. Commonwealth*, 167 Va. 549; 189 S.E. 329 (1937).

[2] *Henderson v. United States*, 237 F.2d 169 (5th Cir. 1956), at 175.

[3] *Sherman v. United States*, 356 U.S. 369 (1958).

[4] Harry Kalven, Jr., and Hans Zeisel, *The American Jury* (Boston: Little, Brown, 1966), p. 321, f. 9.

[5] *Ibid.*, p. 321.

11 ★ Giving Opinion Testimony

OPINION EVIDENCE

The law does not normally permit a witness to give his opinion upon matters concerned in a case. His duty is to testify to facts within his personal knowledge. His opinion does not have any special value to the court and is therefore excluded.

Of course, the distinction between a fact and an opinion is a fine one. When one person says it was "late" another may think it was not. In practice, however, the courts can make a reasonably common-sense division between fact and opinion evidence. Particularly with police officers, the courts are inclined to permit testimony that is mixed fact and opinion, e.g., the apparent age of a person, approximate height, weight, etc. Sometimes this can be most important, as when a policeman is permitted to give an opinion about the speed at which a vehicle was traveling. Nevertheless, in general a witness may not give his opinion.

However, there is an exception to this rule when a witness is qualified as an expert. Some examples of appropriate expertise are very obvious. Thus, a doctor may give his opinion of the cause of death of a person whose corpse he has examined. Clearly, a doctor does not *know* what the cause of death was; he can only apply his expertise to the facts that he ascertained from his post-mortem examination.

The law allows opinion testimony from experts because without it jury decisions would be out of line with scientific knowledge. Although, in theory, the facts are decided by juries in American courts, in practice expert evidence is often conclusive. If a doctor says he has no doubt that a person died from poisoning, there are few jurors who will refuse to believe it. Of course, if more than one expert testifies, and there is a conflict of expert opinion, the jury may be in the odd position of deciding which expert is right, even though it has not a scrap of training that qualifies it to do so.

Disagreements among experts are not uncommon. They often revolve around the most central issues that can arise in a criminal trial. Thus, psychiatrists differ on whether or not a particular suspect was insane at the time of the acts that have been subject to criminal proceedings. Sometimes disagreement can go even further than this, so that two different diagnoses are offered. Thus, psychiatrists differed on whether Richard Speck, the murderer of eight nurses in Chicago in 1966, was "sociopathic" or suffering from "a chronic brain syndrome associated with cerebral trauma." [1] However, a jury is entitled to reject even unanimous expert testimony if it wishes, because the jury is the ultimate arbiter of the truth. In a proceeding to have a man declared a mental incompetent in California, a jury refused to accept psychiatric testimony that the defendant was suffering from "general paresis" and preferred to believe his friends and neighbors who said he was quite sane. [2]

THE POLICEMAN AS EXPERT

In some circumstances, a police officer will qualify as an expert on the witness stand. When he appears for the prosecution, the D.A. will normally warn him in advance that he will seek to have him give opinions as an expert.

Where this is attempted, there may have to be preliminary legal argument in the absence of the jury. The legal rules relating to experts vary widely. If the D.A. wishes to have a police officer testify to his opinion on a road accident, he may have to argue the legal question whether it is *possible* in law to be an expert on road accidents. Some jurisdictions would undoubtedly say it was not. If the court accepted the legal possibility, it might then go on to determine whether the policeman concerned were indeed qualified as an expert. To do so, the court might question the officer in the absence of the jury.

What sort of factors influence a court in deciding whether a witness is an expert? Obviously, foremost among them are expert qualifications. A doctor can be shown to be an expert by proof of his medical training. Indeed, the courts are so used to doctors that it is rare today that the opposition or the court challenges a doctor's credentials and demands formal proof that he is an M.D. Usually he is merely asked to confirm that is so. But where it is sought to show a policeman is an expert, the problem is larger. His claimed expertise will not be of the sort for which diplomas are awarded; it will most commonly be an expertise developed from experience. Then, a policeman who hopes to qualify as an expert in court must be able to show a large experience of the matters about which the prosecution seeks to have him give his opinion. Of course, if he can show that he had formal instruction upon such matters, he will increase his chances of acceptance as a witness. On such qualifications, a patrolman was allowed to give his opinion of the movements of an automobile and a truck that were in collision. He had not been present when the collision took place and therefore could not swear from eyewitness knowledge what happened. Nevertheless, he was permitted in a civil case to swear his opinion about what had happened. He had been a highway patrolman for six years, and had attended a three-month course that gave some attention to road-accident investigation. He had investigated many road accidents.[3]

The categories of "expert" are never closed, and some policemen have been qualified as experts in ways that are somewhat bizarre. Thus, one officer was qualified in a criminal case as an expert on the effects of kicking and stomping a person in the face. Although he had attended no formal course that dealt with this subject, he had investigated many such incidents over his five and a half years as a policeman.[4] In another criminal case, an officer was recognized as an expert in judging the length of time a vehicle had been stationary by feeling the hood. Apparently, from his experiences, he could judge this from the heat of the metal.[5]

GENERAL CONSIDERATIONS REGARDING EXPERTS

If a policeman is qualified as an expert, his expertise will usually be of a narrowly confined kind. His qualification does not entitle him to give his opinion on all aspects of the case. His opinion is accepted only in respect to those matters in which his expertise has been acknowledged by the court. Thus, in the case mentioned on page 154 where the police officer was qualified to give his opinion about the movements of an automobile and truck that were in an accident, the appeal court made it clear that his qualifications could not have been sufficient to allow him to give his opinion about the *speed* at which either of the vehicles was traveling immediately before the collision. To be permitted to give an opinion relating to speed, an officer would not only have to show some experience, but additional special factual evidence, like lengthy skid marks, which would mark out his opinion as expert, rather than as an intuitive guess.

Whatever the nature of the opinion a policeman may give as an expert, a special onus lies upon him to be impartial. One of the reasons that most courts are reluctant to recognize experts is that uncontradicted opinion evidence weighs heavily with juries. When a witness simply testifies to facts, the opposition may show how reliable the witness is by cross-examination. The opposition's right to confrontation is therefore preserved. When a witness is treated as an expert, that right is to some extent diminished. It is impossible to disprove an *opinion;* and if a court has recognized a witness as an expert, it is difficult to persuade a jury otherwise. Thus, an expert witness has a duty to consider any opinion he may have carefully before presenting it from the witness stand.

Because of the considerable influence that expert evidence may have with a jury, courts are generally less willing to recognize expertise in criminal cases than in civil cases; criminal trials may result in the defendant's loss of liberty, whereas civil cases do not.

It should be noted that qualification as an expert lasts only for one trial. An officer who has been accepted as an expert on road accidents in one case may not go into another case claiming to be an expert. If he is to testify in the second trial as an expert, he must be qualified anew. It is perfectly possible that one trial court may recognize his expertise while another will not.

POLICE EXPERTISE IN EYEWITNESS IDENTIFICATION

The previous sections of this chapter have dealt with situations in which a court will make a formal acknowledgement of a witness's expertise. But there are some occasions upon which a policeman may give opinion evidence even though the court does not recognize him as an expert, and yet his testimony will carry special weight. The most important police evidence of this sort is eyewitness identification.

When a witness is asked to identify an accused in the courtroom, he is, in effect, being asked for his opinion. Even though the general rule forbids opinion evidence, identifications do involve a witness's opinion—that the person whom he sees in the courtroom is the same as the one he saw committing an illegal act. Where the witness is a policeman, his identification will usually carry special weight with a jury; it is part of his business to make accurate identifications. "Ninety-nine times out of a hundred, he is more accurate at describing any fast-moving event, such as a murder, a shooting, an accident, than any layman." [6] Similarly, he more quickly absorbs the features of those he observes, their mannerisms, and their special peculiarities. The weight attached to his identification evidence is not given because the court has recognized him as an expert, but because common sense tells the jury that a policeman will be better at identification than the man in the street.

It so happens that identification evidence generally is thoroughly suspect. A committee that investigated a notorious case of wrongful conviction in England concluded that:

> . . . evidence as to identity based upon personal impressions, however *bona fide,* is perhaps of all classes of evidence the least to be relied upon, and therefore, unless supported by other facts, an unsafe basis for the verdict of a jury.[7]

In spite of their training and experience, policemen have been shown to make wrongful identifications; they are not infallible. A writer who made a detailed study of the problem suggested that "although a trained observer is somewhat less likely to make an erroneous identification than the average untrained observer, the mere fact that he has been so trained is no guarantee that he is correct in a specific case."[8]

The police, therefore, have a special responsibility in presenting identification evidence on the stand. They know in advance that a jury will be specially receptive to their identifications and perhaps treat them as experts, although in the strict sense they are not. What measures should a police witness take to ensure that his identifications are fair? He will believe that he "has the right man," of course, and his testimony will be in good faith. Before trial, he should consider carefully all those factors that might cast doubt upon his identification, even though he believes it to be a reliable one. He should note down how long he was able to observe the suspect, from what distance, whether it was dark, whether there was any obstruction that prevented him from seeing clearly, and whether he suffers from poor eyesight. These matters should be brought to the attention of the prosecutor (preferably in advance of trial) in any case where identification will be a question of importance. If this is done, the prosecutor will know how much reliance may be placed upon the identification, and the police witness need not fear that he will be placing undue value upon his own identification. This is definitely a kind of evidence about which a second opinion should be taken from the prosecutor.

It is by no means unknown for police-officer eyewitnesses to disagree with each other. An example comes from an appellate decision in England. Two police officers had stopped a car that was driven by the accused. Both of them noticed that he had not shaved recently. On the witness stand, one officer thought the accused had not shaved for about three weeks; the other thought it was about three *days*. On appeal, the accused claimed that his conviction should be quashed because the identification evidence was unsatisfactory, but the court of appeal affirmed the conviction on the ground that there was other evidence that the jury, as fact-finder, might rely on to establish identification beyond reasonable doubt. The court acknowledged that the discrepancy between the two officers' opinions cast some doubt, but did not believe that it justified interfering with the jury's verdict.[9]

This case illustrates that expertise does not mean uniformity; experts may legitimately disagree. It also shows that a disagreement between police witnesses is not fatal to the prosecution.

NOTES

[1] Jack Altman and Marvin Ziporyn, *Born to Raise Hell* (New York: Grove Press, 1968), pp. 187–188. This difference of ex-

pert opinion was never presented to a jury, because Speck's counsel chose not to raise the defense of insanity. Speck was convicted of all eight murders.

² Jerry Giesler, *Hollywood Lawyer* (New York: Pocket Books, 1962), p. 260.

³ *Hernandez v. Anderson Trucking Co.*, 370 S.W.2d 909 (1963), at 911. (Civil Court of Appeals of Texas.)

⁴ *Morris v. State of Texas*, 373 S.W.2d 495 (1964), at 497.

⁵ *Johnson v. State of Texas*, 355 S.W.2d 191 (1962), at 192.

⁶ Adela Rogers St. Johns, *Final Verdict* (New York: Bantam Books, 1964), p. 171.

⁷ Eric R. Watson, *The Trial of Adolf Beck* (Edinburgh and London: William Hodges & Co., Ltd., 1924), p. 250.

⁸ Patrick M. Wall, *Eye-Witness Identification in Criminal Cases* (Springfield, Ill.: Charles C Thomas, 1965), p. 16.

⁹ *R. v. Appleton*, October 11, 1968, *The New York Times*. (Receiving stolen goods.)

12 ★ The Policeman in the Civil Courts

THE DISTINCTION BETWEEN CIVIL AND CRIMINAL CASES

There is no clear-cut distinction between civil and criminal cases, though in practice lawyers find no difficulty in telling the difference between the two. The famous eighteenth-century commentator Blackstone dealt with the subject as follows:

> Wrongs are divisible into two sorts or species, private wrongs and public wrongs. The former are an infringement or privation of the private or civil rights belonging to individuals, considered as individuals, and are thereupon frequently termed civil injuries; the latter are a breach and violation of public rights and duties which affect the whole community considered as a community; and are distinguished by the harsher appellation of crimes and misdemeanours.[1]

The trouble with Blackstone's attempted distinction is that it does not tell us how to recognize whether, in any given instance, we are dealing with a civil or a criminal wrong. The practical distinction is that civil suits generally result in awards by the court that are not *designed* to punish, whereas criminal sentences are designed to punish. Thus, in a civil suit and in a criminal case, the defendant may be required to pay over a sum of money. But the civil judgment is given because the defendant has been found to *owe* that money, whereas the money paid under a criminal court's fiat, known as a fine, is designed to punish.[2]

Of course, the same facts may give rise to both criminal and civil liability. For instance, a criminal assault may also constitute a civil assault for which the victim may recover damages. A lawyer knows which kind of action is being brought in such a case by looking to see what sort of order the court is being asked for (one designed to compensate or to punish?); which court the action is being brought in; and whether the case has been brought by the state or by a private individual. The state alone may bring criminal actions.

The civil wrongs that are most nearly like crimes are called *torts*. Torts are civil wrongs other than breach of contract for which courts will give a remedy. It is generally agreed that an exact definition of tort law is impossible, because the various actions the courts recognize are more or less unconnected.[3] The most common tort action is one for *negligence*, and nearly all civil actions arising out of road accidents allege the tort of negligence.

Where a set of facts raises the possibility of criminal and civil liability, it is often chance or custom that decides what sort of proceedings will be instituted. Under the common law, civil proceedings could not be brought until criminal proceedings were completed, but that rule has been abandoned in most American states, so that there is a choice. Although a robbery almost always constitutes at least two torts —assault and conversion—very few robbers are sued in tort, because if they have been found guilty, they will be in prison, and in practice not worth suing. On the other hand, false imprisonment is a crime, but it is so rarely prosecuted that this book deals with it exclusively as a tort.

WHEN AN OFFICER SHOULD ACT AS A WITNESS IN A CIVIL CASE

When a civil action arises and a police officer has been a witness to some material event, he will be a highly prized witness for one side or another. His status will lend his testimony weight in a civil case. Indeed, because he has no professional interest in the outcome of a civil case, he may be more readily believed in a civil action than in a criminal one.

Since he is a valuable witness, a police officer should never *agree* to appear for one side or another in a civil dispute. If he does, he may give the impression that he favors the side he agrees to testify for. Instead, he should wait until he is subpoenaed. In that way, he avoids the accusation that he, or the police department, has shown favor in appearing on behalf of a party; the subpoena is a court order that he shall appear, and therefore he has no choice. Some police departments expressly prohibit their officers from acting as civil witnesses unless they are subpoenaed,[4] but even in forces where there is no such rule, an officer should not appear unless required to do so.

THE POLICEMAN AS DEFENDANT
IN A CIVIL ACTION

We have so far discussed civil actions from the point of view of a police witness. Of course, a police officer may have a more intimate connection with a civil case than that; he may be a defendant. His job brings him into situations that can easily burgeon into a civil action. In consequence, a police officer must be acquainted with the major forms of tort that may be alleged against him.

A police officer who is a defendant suffers special problems. First, his career may be at stake; he has a strong incentive to defend himself vigorously. A corporation president who is sued for assault may not suffer any professional consequences if he is held liable. A police officer, on the other hand, may be subject to a wide variety of professional sanctions—suspension, loss of rank, even dismissal from his force. Second, almost any tort action brought against a policeman will develop emotional tensions in the course of trial. It will lead to what lawyers call "hard-swearing"—both plaintiff and defendant taking very definite and contradictory positions. Almost any action brought against a police officer is in substance an allegation that he has abused his authority. The heat generated by any such case will be considerable. This is particularly so where the plaintiff belongs to a minority racial group. A plaintiff may exploit the sympathy customarily given to the underdog in his appeal to the jury.

In the face of these particular problems, a police officer should be specially temperate in his courtroom demeanor. In a civil case, he will almost certainly enter the witness-box on his own behalf. At all costs he should avoid any appearance of vindictiveness or bias.

In many instances, a tort action against the police will necessitate calling several police officers as witnesses for the defense. Unfortunately, however good their testimony may be, it cannot be relied upon to impress a jury. This is particularly so because a jury instruction may be given to the effect that a police witness has a vested interest in "backing up" a fellow employee of the police department, and therefore issues of credibility are involved.[5]

For many officers, civil actions against the police department are especially annoying. They regard them as unfair and often malicious. However, they should not forget that almost all professional men suffer similar risks. A doctor or a lawyer may be sued for negligence. Indeed, there is a word lawyers apply to suits against professional people—"malpractice." There is no tort of the name "malpractice"—but it is a convenient term to describe tortious actions that arise out of professional conduct. Just as a doctor or lawyer assumes the risk that he will be sued for malpractice of one kind or another, so does a police officer. He will naturally seek to avoid liability, and if his conduct as a policeman has been proper, he will do so.

Of course, this advice presupposes that the civil action has come to trial. An officer should remember that it is possible to settle a civil action. This has special advantages for a police defendant, because it avoids unwholesome publicity for the police department. If there seems to be substance in the plaintiff's complaint (and no police department can be infallible), settlement will be an appropriate solution.

The actions most frequently brought against the police involve the torts of deprivation of rights under the Civil Rights

Act of 1871, false imprisonment, assault and battery, and defamation.

ACTIONS AGAINST THE POLICE UNDER THE CIVIL RIGHTS ACT OF 1871

The most wide-sweeping action that can be brought against the police is under the Civil Rights Act, 1871, section 1983, which provides:

> Every person who, under color of any statute, ordinance, regulation, custom, or usage, of any State or Territory, subjects, or causes to be subjected, any citizen of the United States or other person within the jurisdiction thereof to the deprivation of any rights, privileges, or immunities secured by the Constitution and laws, shall be liable to the party injured in an action at law, suit in equity, or other proper proceeding for redress.

Although this provision does not specifically single out policemen as defendants, it is nevertheless true that in a large number of the successful suits under this section, the defendants have been police officers. The reason is clear: the police work in constitutionally sensitive areas all the time and are therefore vulnerable to an accusation that they have deprived someone of his rights.

In the leading case involving this section, *Monroe v. Pape*, 365 U.S. 167 (1961), it was held that the plaintiff need not show a specific intent to deprive him of his constitutional rights. Thus, a police officer will have no defense against such an action if he did indeed deprive the plaintiff of his rights. It will be seen that the wording of section 1983 is therefore very wide. Not only is there no requirement that specific intent be shown, but there is much room for argument about what rights are secured by the Constitution.[6] Thus, successful actions have been brought against the police under this section for widely different reasons. A woman sued the police for taking and distributing photographs of her in the nude after she complained to them of assault. The police defended on the grounds that the photographs were taken to preserve evidence of body bruising, but finally settled the case for $1,250.[7] In the *Monroe* case, the plaintiff was a Negro whose house was illegally searched and who was illegally detained at the police station for ten hours. It should be noted that the *Monroe* facts would probably also have justified an action in the state courts for false imprisonment, but the action under section 1983 may be brought regardless of whether state remedies exist and whether they have been exercised.

Under section 1985 of the 1871 Act, a conspiracy with the purpose of depriving a plaintiff of equal protection of the laws is also actionable.

In general, the amount of damages in successful actions' under sections 1983 and 1985 does not appear to have been high. This is so even though exemplary or punitive damages are permitted in such actions. A police officer who finds himself a defendant in such an action must obviously confine himself to a statement of how the complained-of acts took place. It is not open to him to dispute on the witness stand whether the plaintiff was deprived of his constitutional rights; that, if it is to be disputed at all, will be done by his lawyer.

FALSE IMPRISONMENT AND FALSE ARREST

False imprisonment is wrongful detention of a person. The question arises: What amounts to "wrongful" detention? It may be of three types: (1) wrongful arrest without warrant; (2) arrest on an illegally issued warrant; (3) arrest on a legally issued warrant that has been wrongfully executed. Of course, these categories all raise problems in the law of arrest, with which police officers are already conversant. This section deals only with the civil action for false imprisonment as it affects courtroom testimony.

More than any other type of action, false imprisonment challenges the propriety of an officer's conduct. If he is a good policeman, he need have nothing to fear from the action, because he will be able to justify all his actions, and therefore the plaintiff will lose. A mistake too frequently made by officers who have been named defendants in a suit for false imprisonment is to overstate their case on the witness stand. No policeman should exaggerate the facts in order to defend himself from an allegation of false imprisonment.

The law is lamentably vague with regard to arrest, with or without warrant. True, the standards are easy to state in the abstract—"probable cause" and such terms are common parlance—but what they mean in practice leaves room for doubt. Like all legal concepts, there is an area left in real life for dispute about whether probable cause existed. In the first form of false imprisonment (1, above), an officer should merely state on the witness stand what, in his professional opinion, gave him probable cause for arrest. The second form (2) need not greatly concern him, because if he acts under protection of a warrant, he is normally protected legally; the magistrate or judge who issued the warrant has given authorization, which is sufficient defense in law. However, an officer should remember that protection under a warrant may be lost if he *induced* the issuance of the warrant by telling the judge a story which was not substantially accurate. The third category (3) of false imprisonment actions can raise difficulties; but most officers will experience no doubt in executing a warrant, and this is a rare sort of action. The golden rule is to follow exactly the instructions which appear on the face of the warrant. Most false imprisonment actions that challenge the manner of execution of a warrant do so on the ground that the executing officer has gone beyond the authority of the warrant.

Although the police resent false imprisonment actions, they are quite well protected from unfair verdicts. For example, in most jurisdictions honest belief in reasonable cause for detention is a defense.[8] On the plaintiff's side, by contrast, a false imprisonment action may succeed without proof of actual damage.[9] In this, false imprisonment differs from most tortious actions. The reason is that society has an interest in containing the police in their interference with a citizen's liberty.

The words "false imprisonment" are archaic and misleading. *False* is archaic because a better word would be "wrongful," or "illegal." *Imprisonment* is misleading, because the detention required to prove the tort is not necessarily within a prison. Any bodily restraint is sufficient, e.g., holding a person down, so that he cannot get away, or locking him in a room.

An officer who is unlucky enough to be a defendant in an action for false imprisonment may feel that his professional career is at stake. This is not true; all professional people must rely on their judgment, and they all on occasion misjudge a situation. Furthermore, the mere fact that an officer's action is challenged in court does not mean that he has done anything wrong; a policeman, like anyone else, is presumed innocent until proven guilty. If the decision goes against him, he will have the consolation of knowing that his case is a rare one; most false imprisonment actions are hopeless and brought merely as a harrassment against the police.

In practice, a conscientious officer need have nothing to fear from this kind of action, because any detaining he does will be justified according to normal principles of arrest. If he faces a court, however, he should answer its questions with the maximum of frankness, so as to avoid giving the impression that he is a totally "bad cop." If a jury senses that a policeman is "bending" his testimony in order to make his action sound more reasonable than it was, it may conclude that the plaintiff did indeed fall into bad hands.

There is one interesting question raised by the false imprisonment action, which points to the care with which a police officer should advise the public. Suppose that a citizen, X, thinks that he has reason to arrest another citizen, Y. X consults a police officer about the situation. On the facts that X tells him, the police officer advises that X may make a "citizen's arrest" of Y. X thereupon does so. Y later sues X for false imprisonment. May X defend himself by saying that the police officer advised him that it was all right to arrest Y? The position, according to one English

case, is that X has a defense.[10] What is at present unde-
cided is whether, in those circumstances, the police officer
would be liable for the false imprisonment if X sued him.
While the problem is unresolved, a policeman should beware of advising in favor of a citizen's arrest.

Theoretically, false imprisonment may be prosecuted
by the state as a *crime*, as well as a tort, but this has been
rare in modern times.[11]

False arrest is very similar to false imprisonment. It involves an allegation that an arrest was unlawful because
there was no probable cause for it. This is a subject with
which all police officers are familiar and will therefore not
be dealt with in detail here. It should be noted, however,
that even a lawful arrest may be followed by a false imprisonment. If the arrest was justified at the time, but
subsequently turns out to have been mistaken, a police
officer must release the arrestee. If he does not, a false
imprisonment has been committed.

ASSAULT AND BATTERY

The definition of the torts of assault and battery is
identical with the crimes of that name. They are therefore
not discussed in detail here.

The tortious allegation against the police can arise
where a member of the public believes that the police
have acted with *excessive* force in the execution of their
duty. Like most allegations against the police, it is one
easily made but less easily proved. A defendant police
officer should seek to show the reasonableness of his actions in the circumstances with which he was faced.

DEFAMATION

Many officers will be surprised to see defamation dealt with as a tort for which the police may be held liable. Nevertheless, a policeman's job renders him specially vulnerable to defamation actions. First, as noted in Chapter 15 (*Publicity and Testimony*), he may be responsible for making statements to the press. Second, much of the information he deals with is of a kind that most people wish to conceal. No one wants it to be known that he has been arrested, or convicted.

There are two types of defamation—libel and slander. Broadly, libel is the result of writing, and slander the result of the spoken word. The essence of the tort is that a person's reputation has been unjustifiably harmed. To say that someone is a criminal is defamatory because it lowers him in the eyes of the community at large. However, if he is a criminal he cannot successfully sue for slander, because he is not entitled to a better reputation than he deserves.

Most communications the police make in the course of their duty are "privileged"—that is to say, regardless of their truth or falsehood, they cannot give rise to a defamation action. They are privileged because they are communicated between a person who has a legitimate interest in the matter to someone else who has such an interest. Precisely what interest will be accepted by the courts is somewhat controversial, but it certainly covers communications between police officers investigating a crime. The only instance in which privilege between police officers will not exist is where the communication of false information is malicious, i.e., is not done in good faith. Then, regardless of what legitimate interest in communication there might have been, the privilege is lost by abuse.

However, a police officer comes into possession of a great deal of information that the public may find of interest. He should remember that if he tells of his experiences in the force, or recounts information that he obtains from having been in the force, then what he says is not privileged, unless he is acting in the course of his police duty. In other words, if he tells his story for the sake of its interest or entertainment value, and it happens to be defamatory, he will have no defense.

A famous English case illustrates the danger of such talk. A well-known retired detective wrote his reminiscences for a newspaper. He dealt with a case in which a man had been convicted of robbery. Even after his conviction, the man had consistently maintained that he was innocent of the crime. The detective wrote in his newspaper articles his firm belief that the man was guilty and had properly been convicted. The convicted man thereupon instituted proceedings for libel against the detective, which he won, and he received $3,500 damages! The English law does not accept a conviction as conclusive evidence of guilt in subsequent civil proceedings. The jury in the libel trial believed the convict and hence was entitled to find against the defendant-detective.[12]

Oddly enough, there seems to be no action in the United States that has decided whether a conviction may be treated as conclusive evidence of guilt in a subsequent civil action. There is an old decision that holds that no libel is committed by saying that someone has been convicted of an offense if indeed he has been, whether or not he is actually guilty.[13] However, that is not precisely the same as the English case, because where it is said that a person has been *convicted* of an offense, it is literally true. It is a different thing to assert that a person is not only convicted but also in fact guilty. However, a policeman may feel that discretion is the better part of valor and avoid any controversy about whether a conviction was a just one.

CIVIL PROCEEDINGS THAT REQUIRE SPECIAL TECHNIQUES

Apart from torts, there are special types of civil action in which a policeman may have to testify, which, because of their subject matter, require special tact.

DIVORCE AND OTHER MATRIMONIAL ACTIONS

An officer may become a witness in divorce proceedings in which he has some knowledge of the troubles of the couple involved. He may be a witness to cruelty or adultery, both of which are grounds for divorce in many states. Sometimes it is part of a policeman's job to protect one party to an unhappy marriage against the other if physical violence develops. Further, some divorce lawyers advise their clients to call the police when a matrimonial dispute arises, so that testimony will be available when suit (for divorce, or separation, or support) is brought.

PROCEEDINGS TO COMMIT
A MENTALLY DISTURBED PERSON

The police frequently come into contact with the mentally ill, because mental illness is often manifested in eccentric conduct. Sometimes relatives or the community take court proceedings to commit such people to an institution against their will. Where an officer arrests someone on probable cause, he may find that the arrestee is a mental case rather than a criminal. In such circumstances, the police department has a choice whether to institute criminal proceedings or a civil commitment. We have little information upon how the choice is made, though a recent writer believes that the police tend "to err in the direction of moving the offender along the criminal route." [14] Normally, civil commitment should be attempted only if a person is an actual or potential public danger, although only a quarter of state statutes on the subject require a showing of danger.[15]

PROCEEDINGS INVOLVING JUVENILES

The juvenile courts for many years pretended that their proceedings were not "criminal" in nature, in spite of the severe penalties that juvenile courts have authority to impose. However, the Supreme Court, in *Gault v. Arizona*, 387 U.S. 1 (1967), held that a juvenile was entitled to due process of law when before a juvenile court, which means that he is entitled to counsel and confrontation with his accusers. In *Gault* itself, a fifteen-year-old boy had been sentenced to six years' imprisonment for allegedly making obscene telephone calls to a neighbor, and yet at the hearing the neighbor was not called as a witness. Since the *Gault* decision, juvenile courts have followed a procedure similar to that of adult criminal courts, but because of their historically "non-criminal" position, they are mentioned here.

There are also, in some states, truly civil proceedings that may be taken against a juvenile by which he may be put into responsible hands if his parents are unsuitable or he is an orphan. The "responsible hands" are either foster parents or an institution for children. As in the case of the mentally ill, the police have a large discretion; only a quarter of the juveniles arrested by the police are referred to the juvenile courts.[16]

In all three of these special areas—divorce, proceedings involving the insane, and proceedings involving the young—police testimony should be completely neutral and non-vindictive. In particular, all personal opinions about the proceedings should be kept out of testimony.

NOTES

[1] William Blackstone, 3 *Commentaries on the Laws of England*, 2.

[2] There are a few exceptional civil actions in which the plaintiff may ask for *punitive* damages, i.e., a sum of money from the defendant greater than the amount that the plaintiff has suffered from the defendant's action. These are rare and in practice will not concern an officer, but it is worth noting that such actions are designed to punish, even though they are civil.

[3] See William L. Prosser, *Handbook of the Law of Torts*, 3rd ed. (St. Paul, Minn.: West Publishing Co., 1964), p. 1: "A really satisfactory definition of a tort has yet to be found."

[4] E.g., *Rules and Regulations for Police Department of Den-*

ver, Colorado (1956), p. 42: "Officers shall not testify in civil cases unless legally summoned."

[5] See, for such a jury instruction, 15 *Am. Jur. Trials* 717.

[6] For a collection of actions brought under section 1983, see 15 *Am. Jur. Trials* 580–590.

[7] *York v. Story,* 324 F.2d 450 (9th Cir. 1963).

[8] *Bapuji v. Mooney* (1966) C.L.Y. 7577. This English case is cited because false imprisonment is an old established common-law action. The common law originated in England, and most states of the Union follow the common law.

[9] William L. Prosser, *Handbook of the Law of Torts,* 3rd ed. (St. Paul, Minn.: West Publishing Co., 1964), pp. 55–56.

[10] *Malz v. Rosen* (1966) 1 W.L.R. 1008.

[11] For a discussion of false imprisonment as a crime, with citations to many of the American cases, see Melvin F. Wingersky, *Clark & Marshall's Law of Crimes,* 6th ed. (Chicago: Callaghan & Co., 1958), pp. 664–667.

[12] *Hinds v. Sparks* (1964) C.L.R. 717.

[13] *Hanson v. Bristow,* 123 P. 725 (1912) (Kansas). See also *Mattheis v. Hoyt,* 136 F. Supp. 119 (1955).

[14] Abraham S. Goldstein, *The Insanity Defense* (New Haven: Yale University Press, 1967), p. 174.

[15] *Ibid.,* p. 173.

[16] Ruth Shonle Cavan, *Juvenile Delinquency* (Philadelphia: J. P. Lippincott Co., 1962), p. 239.

13 ★ Dealing with Prospective Witnesses

This chapter deals with police relations with members of the public who have valuable information that may be used in court. The police are the first officials to get in contact with those with information, and their influence may be crucial. True, the district attorney will direct any necessary search for witnesses once it has been decided to prosecute—but that gives the police little guidance in handling prospective sources of information and testimony prior to the decision to prosecute. In the early stages of investigation the police are on their own. Although the D.A. is "manager" of any criminal proceedings that may go to court, the police must act independently until he steps in. Here there is a contradiction. Although it is the D.A. who decides whether to go to trial, an important factor that he weighs in the balance is the amount of evidence the police have collected before the case comes to his attention. If the police cannot offer him prospective witnesses, he may drop proceedings. Thus, the police should not wait passively for instructions to find witnesses; they should start looking as soon as a crime is reported.

The police have two problems in dealing with members

of the public who have information relating to crime. First, some of these people may not be of the most salubrious sort, particularly petty criminals who turn informer and are therefore suspect in the eyes of a court. Second, even where a crime has been committed publicly, respectable eyewitnesses may be hard to trace and when traced may be unwilling to get embroiled in trial. The police may not wish to put a disreputable informer on the stand, and a reputable member of the public may not wish to put himself there.

INFORMERS

Every modern force uses informers. They are the link between law and the underworld, whose tips are often essential to detecting crime. Yet their use causes the police difficulties, because they are rarely willing to appear in court as prosecution witnesses and the police wish to protect their identity so that they can continue passing on useful material. If they appeared in court, they might be subject to reprisal and would certainly not be taken into the underworld's confidence in the future.

Members of the underworld rarely help the police without an ulterior motive; they do so for money, or for forgiveness of past and present violations of the law. A narcotics addict may give tips to the police so that they allow him to feed his addiction without fear of the law. A robber may turn state's evidence against his accomplice in preference to being prosecuted himself with the virtual certainty of conviction and a long sentence. Yet each time the police rely on such witnesses (as they necessarily do), special problems arise. If the informer appears on the stand, his reliability may be in question, and he may arouse the hostility that many people feel against turncoats and informers. A prosecutor may ask prospective jurors on *voir dire* whether they so abhor informers that they would be incapable of giving an informer's testimony its lawful weight,[1] but as we saw in Chapter 7, pages 85–86, this does not ensure that jurors have an open mind, since a prejudice may not be admitted on *voir dire* even though it exists.

If the informer does not appear in court the police must nevertheless reveal their reliance on him, which again raises important legal issues, and somewhat tarnishes the public image of the department.

INFORMERS WHO APPEAR IN COURT

An informer who becomes a court witness will be somewhat suspect anyway. The defense will attempt to diminish his credibility by harping upon his disloyalty to the accused, or the surreptitious way in which he obtained his information. His connection with the police will be highlighted in order to undermine his good faith; one court remarked while dealing with an alleged evasion of liquor taxes that "the credibility of a policeman's decoy is invariably accepted with a certain amount of skepticism."[2]

Thus, even without payment, informers tend not to enjoy the highest status before the courts. Where they are paid for their services, including courtroom appearance, they may be utterly discredited. The mere fact that they accepted payment, rather than reported what they knew from disinterested public spirit, will be used by the defense to suggest that an informer does nothing without being paid for it, but will do anything for money. This attitude presents the police with a serious dilemma: if they do not pay for information they will not get it, yet if they do pay and subsequently produce their informant in court, his testimony will be undermined by the fact that he is paid. A paid police witness may be asked about his payment in court, just as an expert witness may be, because "a witness's possible financial stake in the particular case is highly relevant." [3] His financial interest in the proceedings affects his credibility.

In spite of these disadvantages in using paid informers, most police departments find it worthwhile. There is no way of avoiding attacks on informers' credibility, but certain methods of payment should be avoided. The cardinal rule is that an informer should be paid whether or not his information leads to conviction. To make conviction the contingency upon which payment depends plays into the hand of the defense, which will argue that the informer has an incentive to doctor his evidence in order to enhance the chances of conviction. It is probably just as effective to base payment upon information that justifies prosecution, or indeed to have no fixed criterion of payment. Then, an informer has a less visible incentive to trim his evidence. For similar reasons, an informer should never be paid on a scale that rises with the seriousness of the charges brought against an accused.

INFORMERS WHO DO NOT APPEAR IN COURT

When informers do not appear in court, the police bear the brunt of the defense attack upon the informer's reliability; since the defense cannot attack the informer himself, who is behind the scenes, it will raise the issue of credibility through its cross-examination of policemen who take the stand and in pre-trial motions that seek to dismiss prosecutions because the informer's information did not give the police probable cause. Probable-cause questions arise when the police have acted, with or without a warrant, on the information of an informer.

WITH WARRANT

An affidavit sworn to obtain a warrant may rely on information received from an undisclosed informer, but if it does, it must include a statement of how the informer knows what he claims to know and why the police consider him to be reliable.

The leading case is *Aguilar v. Texas,* 378 U.S. 108 (1964), in which a search warrant was issued in a narcotics investigation. The Supreme Court there approved an affidavit (which is set out in the law report), which recited that the informer had purchased narcotics from the occupants of the premises to be searched and that on previous occasions information from the same informer had proved correct.

This, of course, is a relatively simple situation, where the police generally know the procedure, but it is unclear what should be done where the police wish to act upon information received from a person who has never before given assistance. The police should in this instance consult the district attorney for advice in drawing up the affidavit, but we may presume that such factors as the following might establish that the new informer's words gave the police probable cause; that the new informer was introduced to the police by an already established informer who was reliable; that the informer had no motive for giving false information and had been warned of the consequences of misleading the police; that the informer was of known good character; that from other evidence in police hands, his story may be partially corroborated.

WITHOUT WARRANT

When the police act on informers' tips without a warrant and a probable-cause hearing follows, the informers' names can be withheld providing that the suspect is not deprived of a fair hearing by not knowing the names. In *United States ex. rel. Coffey v. Fay*, 344 F.2d 625 (1965), a man had been arrested without warrant on a charge of burglary, of which he was later convicted. He challenged the F.B.I.'s right to arrest him on the facts. An F.B.I. agent had got an informer to make a telephone call to the suspect, which the agent was permitted to overhear. The informer had arranged a meeting with the suspect and others at a railroad station next day and the agent arrested the suspect when he kept the appointment.

The accused claimed that he should have been told the identity of the informer, but the court disagreed; the informer was not the source of the information upon which the F.B.I. agent acted, and therefore the informer's credibility was not an issue. Furthermore, the substance of the telephone conversation was corroborated by the fact that the accused did indeed turn up at the railroad station. The accused had not been prejudiced by failure to disclose the informer's identity.

Thus, identity is important only where credibility is in issue; whether credibility is an issue depends upon the facts of each particular case.

COURT AID TO POLICE USE OF INFORMERS

The courts have always aided the police in using informers, and their attitude toward them has never been so hostile as that of the general public, which historically treated informers with scant sympathy.[4] The courts, partly to protect police sources of information and partly to prevent public hostility against informers from being directed against those named in court, have always accorded them a privilege of anonymity:

> The purpose of the privilege is the furtherance and protection of the public interest in law enforcement. The privilege recognizes the obligation of citizens to communicate their knowledge of the commission of crime to law-enforcement officials and, by preserving their anonymity, encourages them to perform that obligation.[5]

The privilege has its roots in an age when there were no policemen and those with information went straight to the local magistrate with their tale. Nowadays, when full-time police departments have taken over the role informers played in those days, the contact between the informer and the police has replaced contact between the informer and the courts. Thus, it is important that a police department understand the law on this subject, which may vitally affect the quality of courtroom testimony.

Ancient law also made provision for payment of informers, by setting aside a proportion of the fine imposed on the criminal, or some of the property escheated from him. Today, informers tend to be paid informally, because, as explained on page 180 of this chapter, the principle of giving an informer a vested interest in conviction has been discredited.

ORDINARY WITNESSES

From informers, we turn to ordinary citizens who happen to have useful information but do not wish to "sell" it to the police. This latter class of witness accounts for the huge bulk of non-police testimony in court. The onus of finding these witnesses falls upon the police, and it is a considerable one. Too many members of the public do not wish to become embroiled in a trial; they have heard that being a court witness is a time-consuming job, with little or no compensation. They do not wish to disrupt their ordinary working lives by attending court unless their own personal interests are at stake.

Although witnesses may be compelled to attend court and give evidence, in many instances they cannot be traced in order to be subpoenaed, because their identity is not known. The public at large simply do not come forward with their information; thus, thirty-eight people heard the cries of help of a murder victim in Queens, New York, but took no step to get in touch with the police at the time or after news of the murder appeared in the papers; they waited for the police to approach them.[6]

Since without witnesses there is no case, the police must devote much of their effort prior to trial to ferreting out witnesses.

Where the matter being investigated took place in public—such as in the case of an accident—as many names and addresses should be taken at the scene as possible. Where a large crowd saw what happened, time may be better used collecting names and addresses than taking statements on the spot from a few people while everyone else drifts away, to be lost forever. Some officers believe that a "representative selection" of the crowd is enough, but that is not ideal; no one can be sure that the selection *is* representative. If the identity of every member of the crowd were ascertained, a considerable number of variations among their stories might appear. A particular difficulty the police face when a large number of witnesses are involved is that they have no power to arrest them in order to preserve their testimony. The most they can do is to request cooperation, which may be refused. Usually, in such circumstances, the police are too busy to appeal to the crowd's public spirit. This in turn has an influence upon the testimony the police do manage to secure, for the people who come forward of their own accord may be particularly forceful personalities. Occasionally, this turns out to be a disadvantage in a witness, because he is overbearing on the witness stand.

CRIMES TO WHICH THERE ARE NO EYEWITNESSES

Serious problems of proof arise from crimes to which there are no eyewitnesses, either because it happens that no one was present, or because the nature of the crime is clandestine. But the fact that there are no eyewitnesses does not mean that there are no witnesses whose testimony could be useful in court. There may be many who can give circumstantial evidence. As with on-the-spot investigation, speed is the essence of witness-tracing. A hypothetical example will illustrate why. If a burglary takes place on Monday night, the chances of finding a neighbor who remembers seeing someone in the street in the small hours of the morning are much greater on Tuesday than on the following Friday; memories are short concerning matters observed that are not blatantly criminal. Yet it may make the difference between success and failure in court if a witness can be brought forward to say that on the night of the burglary he saw someone fitting the accused's description.

The inhabitants of the neighborhood of the scene of the crime should be questioned about any observations made that could be relevant. Sometimes a public appeal for aid put out by the police department as a whole may bring aid.

UNCOOPERATIVE WITNESSES

The police occasionally encounter persons whom they believe to have valuable information who simply refuse to make any statement. There is nothing the police can do except report their belief that the person knows something useful to the prosecutor. If the prosecutor feels it worthwhile, he can subpoena the witness before the grand jury (or to a preliminary hearing in states where there is no grand jury). There, he may question him under oath, and failure to answer will be contempt. However, this course of action is unlikely to attract a prosecutor, because an uncooperative witness may tell a story under threat of a contempt conviction which damages the prosecution case. This is particularly embarrassing before a grand jury, composed of laymen, because it may persuade them not to indict the suspect; a magistrate presiding over a preliminary hearing will probably not be much affected. But no lawyer likes to "fly blind" with a witness, and in effect a witness cannot really be forced to speak—a striking proof of the legal system's assumption that the public at large will voluntarily aid the administration of justice.

The motives a putative witness may have in refusing to speak are many; perhaps he simply does not wish to get involved; perhaps he is fearful of reprisal if he does tell what he knows; perhaps his own bad experiences with the law have caused him to lose faith in it; perhaps, although he will not make it explicit, he is scared of becoming a suspect himself. In any event, if he is adamant the police have no legal power to make him talk.

COOPERATIVE WITNESSES

The usual problem the police face is to find people who are prepared to come forward with evidence. On the other hand, there are public-spirited people who see it as their duty to give assistance if they can. Even if the information they offer is not useful, they should of course be treated with courtesy by the police.

However, cooperative witnesses can create problems of their own. After bizarre or sensational crimes have been committed, the police receive some offers of aid from cranks. These volunteers have no knowledge of the crime apart from what they have gleaned from the mass media, but seek excitement and attention by "assisting" the police. The most extreme form of this illness leads people to confess to crimes that they did not commit. Unfortunately, the police have to spend a considerable amount of energy in checking such information and become sidetracked from fruitful investigation. Sometimes the imaginations of such people are vivid, and they construct stories that are extremely convincing and thus cause much waste of police effort. It is, however, dangerous not to follow up offers of assistance, even from unlikely sources; two murderers of a whole family in Kansas were traced as a result of information proffered by a prison inmate.[7]

Less extreme police problems arise from volunteering witnesses who, although not suffering from delusions, are over-helpful and keen to participate in a trial. Enthusiastic witnesses may exaggerate their knowledge in order to give their story more importance. Where an officer suspects exaggeration, he should test the volunteer for consistency before his information is treated as reliable. The best test is to ask for several statements at intervals of a week or so, and then compare them. Inconsistency will almost certainly appear if a witness has fabricated details, and any discovery of this sort should be reported to the prosecutor.

All volunteer witnesses should be listed at the station house and a signed statement taken from them, no matter how valueless it appears; its relevance may not appear until considerably after the time it is given.

Finally, an officer should remember that his sympathetic treatment of a witness at an early stage may pay dividends if a case comes to trial. The rapport built up between a good police department and all those citizens whom they contact during the course of an investigation will show in the seriousness with which lay witnesses take their duty. If the witnesses feel that the police have not treated their information with the respect it deserves, they may lose their inclination to aid law enforcement between the time of their first contact with the police and the time of trial. What appeared to be promising testimony during investigation can be turned into useless vagueness by a listless witness who has come to believe the police do not care about his testimony.

NOTES

[1] *People v. O'Neil,* 109 N.Y. 251 (1888).

[2] *United States v. One 1942 Studebaker,* 59 F. Supp. 835 (1945).

[3] *Harris v. United States,* 371 F.2d 365 (1967), at 367.

4 William O. Douglas, *An Almanac of Liberty* (Garden City, N.Y.: Dolphin, 1954), p. 106.

5 *Roviaro v. United States,* 353 U.S. 53 (1957), at 59.

6 A. M. Rosenthal, *Thirty-Eight Witnesses* (New York: Mc-Graw-Hill Book Co., 1964), p. 11.

7 Truman Capote, *In Cold Blood* (New York: Random House, 1965), pp. 159–163.

14 ★ Confessions

The admissibility of confessions must be the most controversial aspect of the law of evidence. The police are directly concerned with recent developments in this area, because obtaining a confession may be the only means by which a jury will be convinced of a suspect's guilt.

JUDICIAL AND EXTRAJUDICIAL CONFESSIONS

At the outset, a distinction must be drawn between judicial and extrajudicial confessions. Judicial confessions are those that are made before a judge, i.e., pleas of guilty. The courts readily accept these as conclusive proof of guilt, in spite of the knowledge that mentally unstable people sometimes admit to crimes they did not commit and in spite of the fact that many guilty pleas are coerced by promise of leniency by the prosecuting attorney. Before the end of Dr. Samuel Sheppard's first trial for the murder of his wife, at least twenty-five people confessed to the killing.[1]

Extrajudicial confessions are those made outside the courtroom. The vast majority that become the subject of litigation are made to the police, though of course they may be made to ordinary members of the public. When we talk of "confession law," we usually mean the law relating to extrajudicial confessions.

It is an oddity of American law that whereas the rules relating to judicial confessions are lax—almost to the point where they do not exist—the rules regarding extrajudicial confessions are very strict. There is no logical reason why they should be, and it leads to some paradoxes. If a man pleads guilty before a court, he will be convicted and sentenced. After conviction, he will find it almost impossible to challenge his conviction. If, on the other hand, a man confesses to the police that he committed a crime and as a result is prosecuted, he stands a good chance under present law of excluding evidence of his confession from his trial.

This chapter deals with extrajudicial confessions.

THE CONSTITUTIONAL BASES OF THE MODERN RULES

The recent decisions regarding confessions have been based upon two constitutional guarantees: the privilege against self-incrimination and the right to counsel. The privilege against self-incrimination is expressed in the Constitution as a freedom from compulsion. The rules currently in force construe "compulsion" very widely, so as to go far beyond physical coercion. The "right to counsel" has been interpreted as not only the right to hire a lawyer, but the right to his services free if a person is indigent. These two constitutional provisions, interpreted generously in favor of accused persons, gave rise to the *Miranda* rule.

MIRANDA v. ARIZONA

Miranda v. Arizona, 384 U.S. 436 (1966), expressed in the words of Chief Justice Warren, held that:

> the prosecution may not use statements, whether exculpatory or inculpatory, stemming from custodial interrogation of the defendant unless it demonstrates the use of procedural safeguards effective to secure the privilege against self-incrimination.[2]

"Custodial interrogation" means "questioning initiated by law enforcement officers after a person has been taken into custody or otherwise deprived of his freedom of action in any significant way."

The procedural safeguards are: (1) before questioning, the suspect must be told that he has a right to remain silent and that, if he says anything, it may be used in evidence against him; (2) he has the right to the presence of an attorney.

THE PROBLEM

The courts have shown an increasing unwillingness to permit suspects to be convicted on the basis of their own statements, except when they actually plead "guilty" in court. The constitutional privilege against self-incrimination does not prohibit a man from condemning himself out of his own mouth; it merely says that he cannot be required to do so. The *Miranda* decision in effect holds that if the police do not caution a suspect that he need not say anything and do not inform him of his rights to counsel, he is being "required" to incriminate himself.

Yet is this so? We have seen from discussing plea-bargaining that guilty pleas in court are induced by promise of leniency in sentence made by prosecuting counsel. About 90 percent of convictions result from guilty pleas, many of which have been induced by plea negotiation.[3] This practice is surely much more coercive than the mere failure of a policeman to advise a suspect of his rights. Indeed, the prosecuting attorney probably has far more authority in the eyes of most suspects than the police. In spite of this, the courts have attempted little control of plea-bargaining. The President's Commission on Law Enforcement recommends the continued use of plea negotiation.[4]

Thus, at present, the police are prohibited from coercing a suspect more stringently than is the prosecutor. Their frustration is understandable, but they may take consolation in the fact that the blatant inconsistency of the courts' position on extrajudicial and judicial confessions cannot long survive. It has been understood for over thirty years that if the police promise a suspect a reduced penalty if he confesses, any confession obtained thereby should be excluded.[5] Why should a prosecutor have authority to do the very thing the police are forbidden to do? A prosecutor has no more authority to promise leniency than a policeman; any sentencing power resides exclusively in the hands of the judge.

A popular alternative principle to the one adopted by Supreme Court decisions is that any confession should be admitted for assessment by the jury if it is given in circumstances where it is likely that it is true. After all, justice resides just as much in convicting the guilty as in acquitting the innocent. A principle such as this would certainly exclude confessions that were induced by physical violence or the third degree, of which, anyway, all policemen nowadays disapprove.

It is sometimes argued that the warning of "right to counsel" protects the poor, the ill-educated, and the ignorant. It must be given, so that the rich and intelligent, who know their rights, are not given an unfair advantage over the underdog. Not only is this argument theoretically dubious, but it is practically incorrect. The courts have never gone so far as to exclude extrajudicial confessions entirely; a suspect may "waive" his rights. Suppose that all accused persons are warned, as required by *Miranda*. Is the effect to shield those least able to protect their own rights? It is not; there will be many suspects who waive their rights and proceed to confess. Yet they are the very people most in need of a lawyer. And what of those who choose to get legal representation? The major, perhaps the only, advice their attorneys will give them is "Say nothing." Thus, the odds against the really foolish have actually been lengthened by *Miranda*. Once they have waived their rights, they have no means of attacking the admission of their confession.

There is another aspect of the *Miranda* decision that suggests that the truly stupid are not protected. The Supreme Court does not expect the police to stop anyone who *offers* to make a confession. The police do not even have to warn him of his rights:

There is no requirement that police stop a person who enters a police station and states that he wishes to confess a crime, or a person who calls the police to offer a confession or any other statement he desires to make. Volunteered statements of any kind are not barred by the Fifth Amendment and their admissibility is not affected by our holding today.[6]

Thus, someone who is truly reckless of his interests may hang himself by his own rope; a less abnormal person will not. Yet should not those who have the self-punishing compulsion to confess spontaneously, without interrogation, be best protected of all?

THE IMPORTANCE OF CONFESSIONS

Estimates of the importance of confessions differ. Judge Sobel of New York made a study that showed that confessions were involved in only 10 percent of cases.[7] Kalven and Zeisel's slightly more recent study showed confessions were in issue in 19 percent of the cases that they studied.[8]

These figures are, of course, interesting, but they do not tell the whole, or even the major part, of the story. There are several considerations that render the percentage of cases in which confessions appear rather unhelpful. First, we know that the criminal cases that are litigated represent only a fraction of all case dispositions. Of those disposed of without full trial, there are many in which there has been a confession. Indeed, without those confessions, the prosecutor would frequently not be in a position to bargain effectively for a guilty plea. Second, the number of confessions obtained varies greatly from crime to crime. Thus, 43 percent of homicides involve confessions, whereas only 1 percent of drunken driving and 3 percent of narcotics cases do.[9] Third, certain types of defense are tantamount to "confessions in fact," but do not appear as such in the statistics. Thus, a plea of entrapment or insanity by an accused amounts to an admission of the forbidden act. Even an alibi defense can become the equivalent of a confession if it is shown to be false. Lastly, confessions play an important role in keeping the police informed about the underworld, even though no prosecution results.

HOW TO COMPLY WITH *MIRANDA*

The *Miranda* decision deals with "custodial interrogation," i.e., questioning a suspect in the station house or some other context which deprives the suspect of his freedom. In order that any confession that is obtained be admissible in the courts, the police must warn the suspect, before they question him, that:

(a) he may remain silent. If he talks, what he says may be used as evidence against him;

(b) he may hire a lawyer, or, if he cannot afford one, he will be provided with one at state expense, and until that is done he will not be questioned.

It is not enough that a suspect merely continue to answer questions after being given warnings. An "intelligent" waiver must be obtained from him; ". . . a valid waiver will not be presumed simply from the silence of the accused after warnings are given or simply from the fact that a confession was in fact eventually obtained." [10]

The waiver must be taken with knowledge of its consequences. After warnings, it may be desirable to ask the accused, "Do you understand the rights that have just been explained to you?" If the answer is yes, the further question should be asked, "Are you nevertheless prepared to talk to us and forego those rights?" If this question is answered yes, it is believed that the waiver is valid. Some police forces have "waiver forms" in use, which a suspect is invited to sign, but although these may be useful, the mere fact that a suspect signs one may not be conclusive from the point of view of the courts. It is probably not sufficient to hand one of these forms to a suspect and say "sign here." Again, the circumstances of the signature must show an "intelligent waiver."

NOTES

[1] Paul Holmes, *The Sheppard Murder Case* (New York: Bantam Books, 1962), p. 202.

[2] 384 U.S. 444 (1966).

[3] *The Challenge of Crime in a Free Society* (New York: Avon Books, 1968), p. 333.

[4] *Ibid.*, pp. 336–337.

[5] See John H. Wigmore, *A Students' Textbook on the Law of Evidence* (Chicago: The Foundation Press, 1935), p. 211.

[6] 384 U.S. 478.

[7] *New York Law Journal*, November 22, 1965, p. 1.

[8] Harry Kalven, Jr., and Hans Zeisel, *The American Jury* (Boston: Little, Brown, 1966), p. 143.

[9] *Ibid.*, pp. 142–143.

[10] 384 U.S. 475.

15 ★ Publicity and Testimony

The newspapers, television, and radio seek a great deal of their material from the police. It is cheap news by their standards—and it has local appeal. Yet publicity may actually affect the outcome of a trial. If the stories carried in the press are sufficiently *prejudicial,* any conviction that is obtained after they appear may be quashed, on the ground that the defendant could not receive a fair trial after the publicity his case received.

There are three major sources of news about crime to which the press may turn: the police, the district attorney's office, and the victim or victims. In most cases, the major source of information is the police department handling the case. Since publicity can enhance or destroy the value of courtroom testimony, some discussion of publicity is necessary here.

TYPES OF PRE-TRIAL PUBLICITY

News is generated by criminal activity at every stage. First, there may be a story involved in the discovery that a crime has been committed—that, for example, a house has been robbed or someone has been attacked. Then the process of detection itself can be newsworthy, especially if the police department provides bulletins reporting its progress. When a suspect is identified, and still more when he is caught, the press wish to know. From then on, the court proceedings will provide a great deal of copy. It is a measure of the importance that the press attaches to crime reporting that it will pay large sums of money for "exclusive" stories about exceptional crimes. James Earl Ray was paid $30,000 for giving information to a journalist about his movements before arrest.[1]

Of course, when a suspect gives a "story" to the press, he usually does so in order to raise money for defense expenses. A defendant who does so cannot very well ask for his conviction to be reversed on the ground that what he told the press prejudiced his right to a fair trial; if such an argument were allowed to succeed, any criminal defendant could insure himself against conviction by telling the press that he was guilty.

WHY PRE-TRIAL PUBLICITY MAY NULLIFY CONVICTION

It might be thought odd that publicity should affect court decisions at all. If a man commits a crime and gets bad news coverage, why should he complain?

The answer is that prejudice may prevent any jury from giving a verdict based on the evidence presented in court. If the jurors have been bombarded with suggestions in the press that John Smith is the suspect, that John Smith committed the crime, they may already have made the decision that John Smith is indeed the guilty man, and regard the courtroom evidence as a mere confirmation of what is already known. As the report on the assassination of President Kennedy put it: "The disclosure of evidence encouraged the public from which a jury would ultimately be impanelled, to prejudge the very questions that would be raised in the trial."

Before the mass media were so massive, the law had an effective means of avoiding such bias. Where particular local sentiment had been stirred up by a crime, it was possible for a criminal defendant to request that his trial take place outside the area in which the crime allegedly happened. This was, in legal terminology, a request for change of *venue*. Venue means "neighborhood," and the essence of the request was to remove a trial from an area where feeling regarding the crime ran so high that anyone charged with it could not hope for an unprejudiced jury to be recruited from there.

A change of venue is no longer an adequate safeguard, because news is so widely disseminated today. Sometimes, a spectacular crime may take place with millions of people watching on television, as when Jack Ruby shot the alleged killer of President Kennedy. Although no situation has arisen where the courts have laid down a firm principle, it seems possible that a crime could be committed that was so sensational and attended by so much inflammatory pre-trial publicity that it would be impossible for any conviction to stand; there would be nowhere within the United States that a conviction could be obtained with an impartial jury.

It might be thought that the procedure described in Chapter 7, pages 82–86, known as *voir dire*, would ensure that a fair-minded set of jurors could be chosen, but this is not considered to be an adequate safeguard. Although defense attorneys are entitled to ask questions relating to what prospective jurors have read of the case in the newspapers, their answers are not conclusive. They may say that they retain an open mind—but the idea of the defendant's guilt may nevertheless have been insinuated to them unconsciously. In this respect, the law's attitude toward pre-trial publicity is similar to many people's attitude toward modern advertising or propaganda; if one sees enough of it, it must influence one's thinking.

Although there is supposedly a "presumption of innocence" in our law, many members of the public do not share that presumption. They assume that if a person is arrested and tried, the chances are that he has done something wrong. The public attitude is understandable. By the time a person faces jury trial, the law has indicated in at least two practical ways that it does not presume an accused's innocence. Arrest normally requires probable cause for belief that a person has committed a crime. After that, for an indictment to issue, whether from a grand jury or by another method, there must be sufficient evidence to persuade the issuing authority that there is a real question as to whether the accused is innocent, which should be determined by trial. Thus, the presumption of innocence arises only when the circumstances are suspiciously indicative of guilt. Most members of the public know this, and the law treats that kind of prejudice as inevitable. To some extent, it is eliminated on *voir dire* but, as pointed out in Chapter 7, questioning cannot be wholly effective in discovering the truly prejudiced.

GUIDELINES FOR PRE-TRIAL PUBLICITY

The courts have not evolved satisfactory rules for avoiding "trial by newspaper," because two conflicting legal principles have been involved in the question. On the one hand, American law has supported freedom of speech and freedom of the press. That principle would impose no limits upon reports and comments about pending cases. On the other hand, the courts have also wished to ensure "fair trial." Faced with the twentieth-century development of the mass media, the courts have not adjusted the balance between these principles. Hence, in several cases in recent years, the press has been fed with prejudicial information, which it has published, and later a conviction has been reversed on the ground that the publicity had made fair trial of the accused impossible. That is a topsy-turvy way of going about things, because if the courts knew that a fair trial was impossible in view of the publicity a case had, it would have been fairer to the defendant not to have tried him at all at that time.

Various organizations have tried to improve the law on this point, and the most influential attempt has been the American Bar Association's program on Minimum Standards of Criminal Justice. The A.B.A. committee approved a draft code of standards to govern public statements by law enforcement officers.[2] It recommended that law enforcement agencies adopt internal regulations about press statements to prohibit a police officer from disclosing to the press a suspect's prior criminal record, whether he had confessed, the identity of prospective witnesses in a pending case, or any opinion an officer may have about the accused's guilt or innocence. If a police department fails to adopt such regulations, the A.B.A. recommends that they be imposed by rule of court or statute.

Of course, the A.B.A. has no power to insist that its recommendations be adopted, but they should at least be useful to an officer who wishes to avoid difficulties.

The A.B.A. is not alone in its belief that pre-trial publicity should be controlled; both the Supreme Court and the President's Commission on Crime have taken the same view.[3]

In *Sheppard v. Maxwell*, 384 U.S. 333 (1966), the Supreme Court reversed a state court conviction for murder, on the ground that publicity given *during* trial was prejudicial enough to have deprived the accused of due process. Among the prejudicial matters the Court took into account were statements made by two police officers at different times during the trial.[4] The police should therefore avoid making prejudicial statements during trial, in case they are grounds for reversal.

Although there will never be any decision on the matter, it is almost certain that the conduct of police and prosecutor after Oswald had been arrested for the murder of President Kennedy would have voided any subsequent trial. We have noted, on page 201, other circumstances surrounding the assassination. A Dallas police captain told reporters that the case against Oswald was "cinched." The district attorney, who should have known better, described Oswald as "the man that planned this murder. . . ."[5] Of course, the legal consequences of these statements never came before a court because Oswald himself was killed by Jack Ruby, but we may be fairly sure that, just as in *Sheppard v. Maxwell*, the Supreme Court would have held that the publicity made Oswald's fair trial impossible.

What is extraordinary about the many cases in which

prejudicial publicity has become an issue is the willingness of the police and prosecutors' offices to give out such information. However much they like to figure in the news themselves, there is no need for them to make prejudicial statements. By following the guidelines of the A.B.A., the police can ensure proper news coverage that will not defeat the ends of justice. To give prejudicial material to the press, or to give nonprejudicial material in a prejudicial form, shows a lack of foresight on the part of police departments and prosecutors' offices that verges upon negligence.

Publicity may affect an officer's performance on the witness stand in two ways: (1) he may be cross-examined by defense counsel on statements made to the press, and (2) it may be used by the defense to show a generalized bias in an officer's mind against the kind of person he thinks the accused to be. For example, an officer who has made comments to the press that disparage men with beards and unusual clothes might be vulnerable in any case where the defendant did have a beard and wear unusual clothes. The officer's opinion would probably not be in defense counsel's hands if it had not been reported in the press.

In Chapter 9, on pages 125–127, the techniques of attorneys who seek to find inconsistency were discussed. The more that is said to the press about the police attitude to a case, the more chance there is that ammunition is unwittingly being given to the defense. A police officer is never obligated to give information to the press, and if he does, careful consideration should be given to its consequences at a later stage.

NOTES

[1] *The New York Times,* November 13, 1968. (Report of proceedings by which Ray sought a delay of the date of his trial, in order that his new counsel, Mr. Percy Foreman, could prepare.)

[2] American Bar Association, *Project on Minimum Standards for Criminal Justice, Fair Trial and Free Press, Approved Draft of Standards* (March, 1968), pp. 4–7.

[3] See *Sheppard v. Maxwell,* 384 U.S. 333 (1966), at 363: ". . . where there is a reasonable likelihood that prejudicial news prior to trial will prevent a fair trial, the judge should continue the case until the threat abates, or transfer it to another county not so permeated with publicity." See also *President's Commission on Crime in The District of Columbia, Report on the Metropolitan Police Department* (Washington, D.C.: Government Printing Office, 1966), p. 50.

[4] One by Detective Chief James McArthur, who said that justice for the deceased "will come into this courtroom through our witnesses," 384 U.S. 346, and another by Captain Kerr, which the press reported under a headline reading "Bare-faced Liar, Kerr Says of Sam" ("Sam" was the accused). 384 U.S. 349.

[5] See Melvin M. Belli, *Dallas Justice* (New York: David McKay Co., 1964), p. 31.

16 ★ Legal Standards and the Police

There has been little sympathy between the police and the courts in recent years; many police officers believe that the Supreme Court has "turned against the police, by which they mean that Supreme Court decisions have made the policeman's job more difficult.

It is therefore important that a police officer have some knowledge of how the courts create law. Police law is unsuited to the case method by which courts lay down laws on a sporadic basis. The field might better be covered by the enactment of comprehensive "police codes" such as exist in many European countries, but it is unlikely that such a reform will take place in America. Furthermore, even where a code exists, there is a need for courts to interpret the codes, and so they still influence police methods to some degree. Police officers who understand the process of court lawmaking are better equipped to anticipate legal decisions than those who are not. This chapter deals with the machinery of judicial lawmaking and some of its insurmountable problems in dealing with police.

DIFFICULTIES IN JUDICIAL LAWMAKING

There are two major difficulties inherent in court attempts to formulate standards for the police. First, the courts have no firsthand knowledge of police work, and second, no one knows what the law is until the courts declare it. The police suffer from both these difficulties.

Some judges have recognized that they make rules in the dark. Judge Lumbard of the Federal Court of Appeals for the Second Circuit has written ". . . the courts have been left to make rules and apply constitutional standards with little, if any, real knowledge or guidance regarding the difficulties which face the police in solving . . . crimes in our crowded metropolitan areas." [1] This situation has arisen in America because (1) the police have never been recognized as a branch of the judicial organization; (2) judges in the United States require no special training, but are picked from the ranks of ordinary practicing attorneys; and (3) the attorneys who become judges have usually not practiced criminal law. Criminal work is not, on the whole, profitable to lawyers; most distinguished judges, when they were practicing attorneys, specialized in such civil matters as corporate, tax, or insurance law. The result is that the judges who decide criminal cases, and hence mold the law relating to the police, have had almost no practical experience of the field. At the moment, out of nine Supreme Court justices, only two can claim much experience of the criminal courts.

The second difficulty—that no one knows the law until after the events have been litigated—is one that inevitably arises in a system where the courts can make new law. The point is illustrated by the *Escobedo* decision.[2] Escobedo was taken into custody on suspicion of murder after the Chicago police had been told that he shot and killed his brother-in-law. They refused to allow him to see his lawyer while they were questioning him prior to his indictment, and the Supreme Court, by a bare majority of five to four, reversed his conviction for murder on the ground that Escobedo had been denied his Sixth Amendment right to the assistance of counsel. Yet the four dissenting judges all believed that the Chicago police had acted properly in the circumstances, and indeed two of them thought that a previous Supreme Court decision, which reached the opposite conclusion, was controlling. It was only in retrospect that the Court pronounced the Chicago police wrong.

Whenever the courts modify the law in a new decision such as *Escobedo,* some group or individual falls a casualty to the legal system. In the sphere of criminal law, the police are particularly vulnerable because their conduct is so frequently in issue. They cannot predict which of the thousands of cases that come before the courts each year will produce a new rule of law.

In a system such as this, no police force can avoid being declared wrong occasionally. The Supreme Court is not consistent in its decisions. Since it takes only five out of nine justices to make new law, a minor shift of opinion or change of personnel in the Court can reverse its own previous decisions. To that extent, the law is uncertain. The police have to accept that their conduct will sometimes be declared illegal by the courts, even though at the time of the actions before the courts there was no means of knowing them to be illegal. Police conduct will quite often lead to a reconsideration of a rule of law.

No officer should feel, when the courts pronounce a new

rule, that it is a reflection upon his testimony. Our legal system has developed in this way largely because statute cannot cope with the volume of new law that is required.

An interesting example of the way in which law is modified through court decision is *Guarro v. United States*, 237 F.2d 578 (1956). A plain-clothes officer struck up a conversation with another man in a movie theater. After a few words had been spoken, the man touched the officer's private parts. The man was charged with and convicted of assault. A previous decision had held that to constitute an assault "threat or danger of physical suffering or injury in the ordinary sense is not necessary. The injury suffered by the innocent victim may be fear, shame, humiliation and mental anguish caused by the assault." [3]

On the stand, the plain-clothes policeman specifically denied that he was hurt, embarrassed, or humiliated by the accused's act. Thus, an appeal was taken on the ground that no assault had been proved in the absence of such feelings. The appellate court decided that there could be an assault without them, but for other reasons reversed the conviction.

Obviously, the police officer who testified was in no sense blameworthy. He had answered questions fairly, and it was no discredit to him that his answers raised a question of law.

THE COURTS THAT CREATE STANDARDS

Most of the famous decisions that lay down legal rules for the police come from appellate courts, which do not actually hear the original trials. They are therefore at least one step removed from the court that first heard the case. They have not heard the witnesses, and formulate their impressions only from the written transcript of the lower courts' proceedings, which is called "the record."

From this follows an important consequence. The judges who hear and decide appeals are by and large insulated from the problems of the police. As explained on page 208 of this chapter, few of the judges at appellate level have ever had much experience of criminal work; the judges who tell the police what to do are frequently quite ignorant of the criminal law field.

In addition, the judges are rarely provided with any data regarding police needs that enables them to make sensible decisions. The President's Commission on Law Enforcement remarked upon a recent decision of the Supreme Court that greatly restricted police freedom to obtain confessions that "neither the majority [of judges] nor the minority had much solid data to go on." [4]

It should not be thought, however, that only appellate courts make new law; first instance trial courts can and do. By trial judges' decisions on the admissibility of evidence, a great many restrictive rules have been pronounced. These rules cannot be challenged, because the prosecutor has no appeal in a criminal case. The result is that the police are put in an impossible position:

> They can follow the lower court decision and abandon the [prohibited] practice, in which case an authoritative decision by an appellate court can never be obtained; or they can continue the practice, hoping that in a future case a trial court will sustain it and that a defendant by appealing will give the higher court an opportunity to resolve the point. The first choice is undesirable because it results in the abandonment of what may be legitimate police practice merely because there is no way of testing it in the appellate courts. The second

choice is equally undesirable for it puts the police in the position of deciding which court decisions they will accept and which they will not.[5]

There is another way in which the police may be stuck with an unsatisfactory lower-court decision. A defendant may be convicted, but fail to take a worthwhile legal point on appeal. If this happens, there will be no consideration of the issue in a higher court, because prosecutors do not appeal from convictions that they themselves have procured. In this respect, the Soviet system, by which a senior prosecutor may press cases on appeal on behalf of convicts who do not litigate their convictions, has some merit.[6]

THE CREATION OF UNCERTAINTY

There is still another major way in which court-made law adds to the police burden. Even where rules have been laid down, they can rarely be specific enough for practical doubt to be eliminated. In *Miranda v. Arizona*, 584 U.S. 436 (1965), Mr. Justice White, one of the four justices who disagreed with the majority ruling on confessions, expressed the problem clearly:

> [The] decision leaves open such questions as whether the accused was in custody, whether his statements were spontaneous or the product of interrogation, whether the accused has effectively waived his rights, and whether nontestimonial evidence introduced at trial is the fruit of statements made during a prohibited interrogation, all of which are certain to prove productive of uncertainty during investigation and litigation during prosecution . . .

The proliferation of legally disputable issues is inevitable so long as courts deal in generalizations. No amount of definition and re-examination can anticipate the particular factual situations with which police have to contend. As Chief Justice Warren said in relation to "stop and frisk" law, "No judicial opinion can comprehend the protean variety of the street encounter [between police and public] and we can only judge the facts of the case before us." [7] Such is the position in almost all adjudications on police conduct.

The likelihood that yet more appeals on points of law will be taken in the future has increased because more defendants nowadays have access to counsel.

DEFENSE ATTORNEYS

Why should an accused person be entitled to a lawyer at all? He is charged with a serious crime only after a great deal of evidence which indicates his guilt has been collected. The most that a lawyer can do is to get his client acquitted by a trick, or on a technicality. Many policemen may ask: What public interest is served by that?

The answer can be given on several levels.

First, we can refer to the basic values that the United States embraces as part of its Constitution. Although the states have an important interest in having the law enforced, they also have an interest in seeing that certain minimum standards of justice are preserved. However obvious it may be to the police that an accused is guilty, the final determination of guilt rests with the court. Until a conviction is obtained, no one can say in positive terms that an accused is guilty. The meaning of "guilty" must include an acceptance that the finding of guilt is made by the court machinery that is set up for its determination. That machinery is highly complex and requires professionals to work it. To deny the right to counsel to an accused person would put him at a disadvantage in presenting his side of the story at trial.

Second, society has an interest, not only in convicting the guilty, but in acquitting the innocent. However much a police officer believes that the majority of persons accused of crime are guilty, he must see that every one of them is not. Mistakes do occur; evidence that appears convincing may crumble in the courtroom.

Third, the community has an interest, not only in convicting the guilty, but in the manner of their conviction. We are no longer satisfied with a judicial process such as the ancient trial by ordeal, because we believe that more reasonable types of proof must be found.

By protecting all these interests, a defense lawyer serves the community as well as the defendant. If a defendant has had a competent defense lawyer, he is much less able to discredit any subsequent conviction.

THE RIGHT TO COUNSEL

In *Gideon v. Wainwright*, 372 U.S. 1 (1968), at 14, the Supreme Court announced that the "right to counsel" mentioned in the Constitution included the right of a poor defendant to have a lawyer at the government's expense. In asserting the existence of this right, the Court was attempting to protect the values and interests of the community, which have been listed in the previous section. The *Gideon* decision involved considerable extra public expenditure on lawyers for poor people, and was criticized by many as "mollycoddling" convicts.

Yet it has always been the case that a defendant may hire a lawyer if he can pay for it. Hence, a big-time criminal was always able to protect his interests in court. Why should the poor accused be at a disadvantage? His poverty is no proof that he is more likely to be guilty than a rich defendant. If there is to be anything approaching equal justice, it is not right that a poor man should be unrepresented in court, while a rich man is.

Another criticism frequently made of the decision is that it was unnecessary. The system had worked without poor persons' lawyers before; why jump in with free legal aid? This criticism, directed not so much to the decision itself, as to the Supreme Court, is unfair, because the system had worked badly before and led to a denial of fair trial in some cases. It was therefore reasonable to attempt reform.

The *Gideon* decision does not insist that a poor person take a lawyer. If he wishes, he may defend himself. It is therefore still possible for an officer to appear for the prosecution in a case where the accused is unrepresented.

TESTIFYING WHEN AN ACCUSED IS UNREPRESENTED

An unrepresented accused presents special problems to all those involved in a case. He has the right to conduct his own case, yet if he is ignorant of the rules of procedure and evidence, he will almost certainly do so badly. In particular, the kind of cross-examination he is likely to conduct will be somewhat looser than that which an attorney or judge might choose.

A police officer faced with this situation should face cross-examination politely and show a cooperative attitude. If the accused goes really wide of the mark, the judge will prevent his line of questioning from continuing. In practice, both prosecution lawyers and the judge allow a great deal of leeway to an unrepresented defendant. Even though since *Gideon* it is a defendant's own fault if he does not have counsel, he is entitled to conduct his defense personally. Thus, he will probably be permitted to ask questions and conduct himself in a way that would not be allowed a lawyer.

A policeman should show sympathy to the unrepresented accused, not hostility. This will impress his fair-mindedness upon the jury. He should not object to answering a question, even though he knows it to be improper. He should leave it to the judge to determine how far the accused may go.

LEGAL THEORY THAT FREES CRIMINALS

One of the most amazing theories American courts have adopted is that if the police have acted badly, any conviction that has been obtained as a result of their conduct may be overturned on appeal. This theory was pithily expressed by a famous judge, Mr. Justice Cardozo: "The criminal shall go free because the constable has blundered." [8]

This theory is applied even where the convict is obviously guilty. There is no attempt to weigh whether police misconduct casts doubt upon the rightness of the conviction. Any misconduct may get the accused's conviction reversed on appeal. Hence, there is a built-in incentive in the system for defense attorneys to paint the police in the worst possible light.

We have already seen that until a court has decided what is misconduct, no one knows what it is. Before the *Escobedo* decision, the Chicago police could not have known that their questioning of suspects without permitting them to see their lawyers would be declared illegal. Therefore, all their efforts to bring Escobedo to justice were in vain. (Since Escobedo's release by the Supreme Court, he has been convicted on other charges.)

The dangers of this peculiar legal principle are obvious; it is discouraging to the police; it gives the police unfairly prejudicial publicity; it encourages defense attorneys to deflect their arguments away from the fundamental concern of the court, which is whether the accused is guilty or not; and it allows criminals to believe that they can get off scot-free. Retrial can rarely be ordered in such cases, because of the rule against "double jeopardy" that no man should have to face trial for the same offense twice. Besides, once a court has ruled police evidence inadmissible, it is often difficult to obtain alternative evidence.

The indiscriminate use of the principle described by Mr. Justice Cardozo has been a constant source of friction between police and courts. As one commentator has put it, "the whole meaning of the exclusionary rule is that Americans have not developed decent police administrative procedures." [9] The result is that the courts are too often trying the police as much as the accused. Although cooperation between police and courts is essential, the system contains a built-in disincentive for the police to treat the courts with candor.

The prospects for the future cannot be counted as good. Even if administrative procedures were developed, the tradition of exclusionary rules is so strong that it is unlikely that the courts will ever wholly abandon them.

INCONCLUSIVE LEGAL ARGUMENT

Many of the most important decisions in criminal law have been highly contentious. The Supreme Court has divided almost evenly on many issues. The result is uncertainty, which creates many problems for the police.

An example of the extreme legal arguments which may gain support comes from *Lucille Miller v. California,* 392 U.S. 616 (1968), which reached the Supreme Court.

A dentist was killed when his car caught fire, and his wife was arrested on suspicion of murder. In order to prevent the police from questioning Mrs. Miller, her attorney set up a 24-hour-a-day watch on her cell. The police therefore checked an undercover agent into Mrs. Miller's cell, representing her to be awaiting trial on a fictitious narcotics charge. Mrs. Miller talked with the undercover agent and told her that "as soon as this mess was over, she planned to take [her children] on to Europe with the insurance money" she hoped to collect from the husband's death. The undercover agent testified to this and other matters at trial. Mrs. Miller was convicted of first-degree murder.

In the Supreme Court, Mrs. Miller claimed that her constitutional privilege against self-incrimination had been violated and that her right to counsel had been circumvented. The Court rejected both of her contentions and affirmed her conviction. Yet four out of the nine justices dissented, and believed that her conviction should have been reversed. Led by Mr. Justice Marshall, the minority thought her constitutional claim good, even though there was no direct coercion.

This case is illustrative of the way in which legal questions may be answered in inconsistent ways; if only one justice had changed his mind Mrs. Miller would be free. Even in a murder case, in which the sentence was life imprisonment, the highest court in the land was split five to four.

There are many objections to dissenting judgments in a criminal case, not least that they cast doubt upon the law's certainty. By a process of logical extension, an argument for completely opposite conclusions can be reached in most areas of the criminal law. The difference between right and wrong is therefore inevitably blurred.

THE EFFECT OF LEGAL STANDARDS ON THE POLICE

Studies were done after the "confession" decisions made by the Supreme Court during the 1960s on the effect of the newly proclaimed standards. They indicated that the police were not greatly affected by the new rules. In some instances, they were found to be violating the law.

The reason for this is that in many cases the police have no intention of prosecuting and therefore do not fear that evidence will be excluded from court. As Chief Justice Warren put it, "regardless of how effective the rule may be where obtaining convictions is an important objective of the police, it is powerless to deter . . . where the police either have no interest in prosecuting or are willing to forgo successful prosecution in the interest of serving some other goal." [10]

There can be no excuse for deliberate breaking of the law by the police. However wrong the rules may be to police eyes, they are still the law; the courts have more right to proclaim the law than have the police. If the rules are foolish, they should be criticized forcefully, but not broken. Since lawbreaking by the police is as great a threat to the community as law breaking by any other section of the population, it should be discouraged as strongly as any.

The legal standards applied to the police are of a special kind. To obtain a confession by methods that contravene current Supreme Court standards is not a crime. The sanction imposed is that such a confession will be excluded from any subsequent trial. There is nothing criminal about violating evidentiary rules laid down by the courts. Nevertheless, the police occupy a special position of public responsibility, like other professions, to obey the law, not because of the sanctions behind it, but because they have no right to place their own opinions above those of the courts.

It is easy for policemen who are opposed to recent court decisions to talk themselves into believing that they are "hamstrung" in discharging their professional duties. The evidence suggests, however, that the police are relatively unaffected by at least one of the major Supreme Court opinions relating to confessions. *Miranda v. Arizona*,[11] which imposed a duty upon the police to issue warnings to suspects about their right to remain silent and the right to counsel, was thoroughly unpopular with the police. Yet a detailed survey of its effect upon police operations in New Haven, Connecticut, concluded that "not much has changed after *Miranda*." [12] The reasons given for this conclusion were two:

first, interrogation had never been very important in New Haven crime-solving, and second, most suspects allowed the police to question them even after being warned of their rights. It seems that the police themselves were under a misapprehension about the necessity for interrogation and its by-product, a confession. We know from other sources that a study of a large number of prosecutions revealed that overall only 19 percent of cases brought to trial involved a confession.[13]

It would be foolish to pretend that court decisions leave the police entirely unaffected. Nevertheless, results of the *Miranda* study do not justify the defeatist attitude that some officers adopted when the decision was announced. It is true that much is wrong with American courts and that the police have legitimate objections to some aspects of the legal system. But the courts have not made the police task impossible. Perhaps the greatest contribution the police can make to law enforcement is to work within the ground rules enunciated by judges, however foolish they may appear. A healing of the rift between police and courts may be easier for the police to bring about by a professional acceptance that they should work within the system than it is for the courts. Professional criminals know that a divided enemy can be conquered, and courts and police are divided today.

NOTES

[1] In *Williams v. Fay*, 323 F.2d 65 (1963), at 70.

[2] *Escobedo v. Illinois*, 378 U.S. 478 (1964).

[3] *Beausoleil v. United States*, 107 F.2d 292 (1939), at 296–297.

⁴ *The Challenge of Crime in a Free Society* (New York: Avon Books, 1968), p. 245.

⁵ *Ibid.*, pp. 345–346.

⁶ John N. Hazard, *The Soviet System of Government,* 4th ed. (Chicago: University of Chicago Press, 1968), p. 184.

⁷ *Terry v. Ohio,* 392, U.S. 1 (1968), at 15.

⁸ *People v. Defore,* 242 N.Y. 13 (1926), at 21.

⁹ Norval Morris, quoted in Martin Mayer, *The Lawyers* (New York: Dell Publishing Co., 1968), p. 196.

¹⁰ *Terry v. Ohio,* 392 U.S. 1 (1968), at 14.

¹¹ 384 U.S. 436 (1966). The decision is discussed further in Chapter 14, pp. 193, 197–198.

¹² "Interrogations in New Haven: The Impact of Miranda," *Yale Law Journal* 1519 (1967), at 1613.

¹³ Harry Kalven, Jr., and Hans Zeisel, *The American Jury* (Boston: Little, Brown, 1966), p. 143.

17 ★ After Trial

Although the rules are designed to ensure that only relevant evidence is presented in court, trials have an Alice-in-Wonderland quality. There are interruptions, adjournments, motions in the absence of the jury, and all manner of seemingly irrelevant inquiries. The total effect is one of confusion. This is heightened for witnesses, because they see only part of the trial in which they are appearing. They are naturally concerned with their own part and tend not to notice what else is going on.

It is the mark of a good police officer that he takes an interest in the whole of a trial, even one in which he has only a small part to play. His facility in dealing with trial work will greatly increase if he finds out what factors influence a trial's result, whether it be conviction or acquittal. If possible, he should note the important characteristics of trials in which he gave evidence. His research will be immensely valuable to him personally and to his police force, for by a careful analysis of his experiences, he will improve his performance and that of his department in future cases. Even where the outcome of a prosecution has been disappointing, there will be lessons to be learned; we all learn by our mistakes.

Where can an officer find the time to study his trial experience? There are few police forces in which an officer is permitted to devote his full-time efforts to preparing cases for trial. Furthermore, most of the technical work of trial preparation is taken over by the D.A.'s office, so that police files on the matter are incomplete. This may change once the recommendation of the President's commission is implemented and police departments have their own legal advisers.[1] But even then—and there are good reasons for thinking it will take some time[2]—a police witness will probably have limited access to the legal adviser's files.

The answer must be, in present conditions, that an officer will have to study the trials in which he has been engaged on his own initiative. This is not ideal, but with the help of this book there is no reason why an individual officer should not be able to analyze his experiences profitably. His practice will encourage his department to take a serious interest in trial work, especially if the officer's effectiveness as a witness is improved.

Many policemen believe the result of criminal trials is determined by chance and that there is nothing to be learned from them. This is wrong; there are always valuable insights to be gained from a trial. An assiduous officer should analyze his experiences on the witness stand, and the trial as a whole. The following suggestions will help him.

THE TRANSCRIPT

A single witness is like one piece of a jig-saw puzzle; until his testimony is connected with others', no picture can emerge. Even a police witness who knows more about a case than the average citizen often has little idea of the total picture as it emerges in the courtroom. Particularly if he has been sequestered,[3] he cannot know at the time he gives his evidence just how important his part is. He can ascertain that after trial, by obtaining a copy of the transcript, the verbatim report of the words spoken in court. Many police departments receive copies of the transcript of all trials in which their men participate. They can always be obtained through the prosecutor or the clerk of the court. From this, he sees how the case unfolded before the court. He can see if other witnesses agreed with him. He can see exactly how his own testimony fitted in with other things before the court.

This last advantage of studying the transcript is one many officers overlook. They feel it is unnecessary to read their testimony in transcript, because that part of the trial is the one they know best; they participated in it. But a witness on the stand is under pressure; he must all the time be thinking of his own answers and constantly on his guard. He has no time to be thinking objectively about the total strategy of his examination and cross-examination. If he reads it later, he will see things that never appeared to him while testifying. It is not unusual for a witness to be surprised when reading his own testimony, because the written record gives him a different perspective on what took place in the court. Memory can play tricks. It can suppress uncomfortable moments and distort reality. The transcript often reminds a witness of answers that subconsciously he would prefer to forget. Just as a person may be amazed to hear his voice played back from a tape recorder, so he may be amazed to read what he said.

Reading the transcript of one's own evidence can be a painful and humiliating experience. One thinks: "If only I hadn't said that . . . ," or, "What a fool I was to fall into *that* trap." But it is precisely these embarrassing realizations that make an officer learn from his experience; having seen the written evidence of his mistakes, he will be more careful to avoid them in his next trial.

Reading a transcript also gives an officer some perspective on the relative importance of police testimony, which will be invaluable to him in every future trial.

GAUGING THE IMPORTANCE OF POLICE TESTIMONY

The importance of police testimony varies according to the nature of the case. In nearly all prosecutions where the alleged crime has no eyewitness, such as burglary, police witnesses are extremely important. Where, on the other hand, there are independent eyewitnesses, the police evidence may provide important and even indispensable "fill-in" facts, but it cannot be said that the police witnesses carry the whole prosecution. An example of this latter class might be a hit-and-run automobile accident, where bystanders can tell the court exactly what they saw and identify the accused's car. The police will probably provide evidence of tracking down the car and testify as to what the accused said upon arrest, but it will be rare that members of the police department have any personal knowledge of the accident in question. If they attempted to testify about it, their evidence would be hearsay and ruled inadmissible.

Police witnesses should bear in mind that it is unusual for a policeman to actually see a crime committed; the chances are that police evidence is ancillary. This does not mean to say that police evidence is unimportant, but it indicates that it can rarely have the dramatic quality of indisputably fixing guilt upon the accused. Unless there has been a true eyewitness to a crime, all evidence of guilt is at best inferential. For an officer-witness to conduct himself as if he actually saw the accused commit the crime when he did not will not serve the prosecution.

Apart from making an assessment of the relative importance of police testimony, what should an officer look for in a transcript?

First, he should examine each of the questions he was asked on the stand, whether by prosecutor or defense, and decide whether he could have given a better answer than the one he actually gave. Generally, answers should be short and to the point. Did any of his answers cause confusion, or require a lot of further elucidation? Were there questions that gave an opportunity to place information before the court that it never got?

Second, a list should be made of all the facts that a police witness managed to give to the court during his examination. He should then consider what other information he had in his possession, and whether it would have been admissible. It is surprising how important facts can sometimes be overlooked by the witness, judge, and counsel.

Third, all testimony from policemen should be compared, in order to detect inconsistencies between members of the police force.

QUESTIONING PARTICIPATING LAWYERS

Another important source of opinion about a trial comes from the lawyers involved, both prosecution and defense.

They frequently have pertinent comments to make, not only about the over-all development of the trial, but about the performance of a specific witness. They, after all, have been intimately involved with the case, and the defense lawyer particularly has had to justify his tactics to his client.

The prosecutor should be an easy source of information and opinions for a policeman to tap, because the prosecutor's office will have had some dealings with him before trial. A keen officer who wants to know the prosecutor's views will usually find that he is very ready to talk. There is no reason why he should not ask about his own personal testimony and whether the prosecutor thought it could be improved.

Defense lawyers pose a greater problem. It is natural that they should not be so ready as the D.A. to discuss a case candidly with a policeman. After all, part of the art of a defense lawyer is to keep the prosecution guessing; if his client has been convicted, he may want to appeal. However, many policemen find that defense counsel are quite pleasant if approached after trial. We have already seen, in Chapter 4, pages 47–49, that defense attorneys are happy to speak with police officers before trial; there is no reason why they should not afterward.

JUDGE AND JURY

The general rule is that a judge does not comment upon cases that he has heard. However, it is at his discretion to do so, and if he chooses to, he may well provide an officer with interesting data.

Questioning the jury is generally frowned upon, although

there are numerous historic instances where it has been done.[4] But again, if a juror chooses to talk about the jury's reaction, a policeman should listen.

THE PRESS

Nearly every big case is covered by some section of the press. The crime reporters are often extremely well-versed in courtroom procedure and technique and are not bound by any rules that might inhibit them from expressing their opinions. Whenever possible their observations should be solicited and recorded.

Incidentally, following press reports of a case is often the fastest way of seeing some of the evidence in print. They will not be complete, as a transcript is, but will probably reproduce the highlights of testimony. These may be valuable in assessing the impact of particular pieces of evidence.

APPELLATE RECORDS

If the defendant has been convicted and taken an appeal a police officer should ensure that he gets a copy of the appellate court's judgment and, if possible, the briefs filed by the defense and the D.A. These will often provide a fresh insight into the trial and can generally be obtained from the prosecutor.

A close reading of any trial transcript will nearly always reveal defects of one kind or another in the proceedings; perfection is rarely achieved. The rules of criminal procedure are designed to lessen the margin of error open to a court, but they cannot eliminate it—trying cases is an art, not a science, and the most carefully contrived rules will not prevent mishaps or reduce human fallibility. Hence, an appellate court will not automatically reverse a conviction because it finds a lower court made a mistake; it will go further and decide whether the mistake was sufficiently serious to make it unsafe for the verdict to stand. If the appellate court decides that the defect in the trial proceedings was such that a possible injustice was done to the defendant, it finds "reversible error." Only serious misrepresentations before the jury will normally cause a conviction to be overturned; there have been cases in which the jury has come back from considering its verdict to ask a question regarding the evidence which the judge has answered wrongly, but the subsequent conviction has been allowed to stand. In the trial of Mark Fein for the murder of his bookie, the jury returned from its deliberations to ask how the attention of the police was first centered on a particular New York apartment, and the judge told them that ". . . the record is not clear as to that specific question. . . ." In fact, the record was clear, as one of the jurors realized, and the judge's mistake was corrected.[5]

The knowledge that mistakes are made even by judges should prevent a police officer from holding either himself, his brother officers, or others to unattainable standards. Although a framework of legal rules governs trial conduct, there are many matters that arise in court which involve questions of style and choice rather than questions of right or wrong. There is a temptation to believe that there is only one proper way to present a case in court, a temptation to which policemen and lawyers alike succumb. Trial attorneys recount their courtroom experiences as if at various turning points in their cases they had no choice in what they did; the pattern was pre-ordained. But this is fallacious, because the same case, given to half a dozen different attorneys to defend, would be handled in six different ways. Similarly, two police officers, equally competent but different in temperament, might present much the same information to a court in different ways. The particular flavor of a trial depends upon the talents and personalities of those who conduct it, and there is no one method to try a case, or to give testimony.

It is his individual accountability which should be uppermost in a police officer's mind when he prepares a case for trial. A police witness should, above all, be dedicated to those principles of even-handedness which our system of criminal justice seeks to uphold. The integrity of our legal processes depends ultimately upon the men who operate them, and the contribution of the police in this respect can be particularly valuable. In any criminal trial, there is a tendency to "take sides"; district attorneys are subject to special pressures and a policeman should bear in mind

> that far too many prosecutors view a trial as a kind of game, and they are so busy planning how to out-wit, out-smart and out-maneuver an opponent that they forget that justice is the sole purpose of a criminal trial.[6]

Naturally, the police want to cooperate with the D.A.'s office, but they should not fall into the error of thinking that prosecutors are always right, or rationalize a desire to "nail" a suspect unjustly; a conviction is a proper result of criminal proceedings only if the evidence supports it, and a policeman should not bend to pressure to embroider his testimony no matter from whom its comes.

The police have a special role in maintaining standards worthy of America in our courts, and a police officer who recounts the unvarnished truth shows himself worthy of the heavy responsibility imposed upon him.

NOTES

[1] *The Challenge of Crime in a Free Society* (New York: Avon Books, 1968), p. 290.

[2] The recommendation of the President's Commission was not new; many police manuals have recognized the advantages of forming legal departments within police forces, yet very few have done so. See, e.g., O. W. Wilson, *Police Planning*, 2nd ed. (Springfield, Ill.: Charles C Thomas, 1962), p. 11.

[3] See Chapter 9, pp. 131–135.

[4] E.g., Adela Rogers St. Johns, *Final Verdict* (New York: Bantam Books, 1964), p. 139.

[5] See William A. Reuben, *The Mark Fein Case* (New York: The Dial Press, 1967), pp. 229, 236.

[6] Edward D. Radin, *The Innocents* (New York: William Morrow and Co., 1964), p. 35.

Index